Dining In-Milwaukee

A Collection of Gourmet Recipes for
Complete Meals from Milwaukee's Finest Restaurants

Carol DeMasters

Peanut Butter Publishing
Seattle

Titles in Series:

Dining In—Baltimore
Dining In—Boston
Dining In—Chicago
Dining In—Dallas
Dining In—Denver
Dining In—Hawaii
Dining In—Houston, Vol. I
Dining In—Houston, Vol. II
Dining In—Kansas City
Dining In—Los Angeles
Dining In—Milwaukee
Dining In—Minneapolis/St. Paul
Dining In—Pittsburgh
Dining In—Portland
Dining In—St. Louis
Dining In—San Francisco
Dining In—Seattle, Vol. II
Dining In—Sun Valley
Dining In—Toronto
Dining In—Vancouver, B.C.
Feasting In—Atlanta
Feasting In—New Orleans

Cover photograph by Michael Skott
Illustrations by Neil Sweeney

First printing, November, 1981
Second printing, December, 1981
ISBN 0-89716-099-1

CONTENTS

PREFACE

Before I moved to Milwaukee, I had heard that it was well known for a number of good restaurants. After living here for ten years, I know that is true. Milwaukee is a family town and so it follows that its family-owned restaurants, for the most part, are the backbone of **Dining In–Milwaukee**. Milwaukeeans love to cook and savor the ethnic recipes that have been handed down in their families for generations. When Milwaukeeans dine in restaurants, they expect and demand good-quality food, and that is why Milwaukee has a long tradition of fine dining.

A few Milwaukee restaurants are approaching the century mark of operation under the same family, having seen succeeding generations come into establishments founded and nurtured by their parents and grandparents. There is a sense of family pride and tradition. Owners say that they are successful because their whole family has a part in the business and operation of their restaurants.

Researching and writing **Dining In–Milwaukee** has been a culinary discovery for me. Meeting and talking with the chefs of Milwaukee's finer restaurants is an opportunity everyone interested in good food and cooking should have. Restaurant owners and chefs have been generous with their prized recipes and never withheld the tips or secrets that make cooking a successful and satisfying endeavor. It is with great pleasure that I am able to share the specialties of some of Milwaukee's finest chefs with the readers of **Dining In–Milwaukee**.

Through my years as food editor at the *Milwaukee Sentinel*, I have learned from the chefs I've interviewed that a recipe, for the most part, is essentially a guide. Chefs add common sense, a feeling for food and cooking and flair to recipes. They urge the home cook to do the same. Practally all of the recipes in this book have been reduced from large quantity versions.

I hope you will enjoy discovering the tastes of Milwaukee with the talented chefs and restaurateurs who have made this book possible.

Carol DeMasters

BARTH'S
at the bridge LTD

Dinner for Six

Sautéed Chicken Livers

Chicken Broth with Parlsey Dumplings

Tossed Garden Salad With Sour Cream Dressing

Beef Burgundy

Sweet and Sour Red Cabbage

Hershey Bar Torte

Wine:

With the Chicken Livers—Madeira or dry Sherry
With the Beef—a light-bodied Beaujolais
With the Torte—Asti Spumante or Cream Sherry

Palmer and Arleen Krueger,
Peter and Linda Krueger, Thomas and Sharon Krueger,
Mary Lou Grosser, Proprietors
Peter Krueger, Chef

BARTH'S AT THE BRIDGE

Barth's at the Bridge is as rich in tradition as the town in which it is located—Cedarburg, just north of Milwaukee. The co-founder of Cedarburg, Frederick Hilgen, settled in the area in 1844. In the 1850s he built a grist mill on the west bank of Cedar Creek which still stands today. Just across the street he built a three-story building to use as a dwelling and as a retail flour and feed store. Today, Barth's occupies this building.

In the 1860s, Hilgen built three hotels and dining rooms and a tavern which were operated as a resort. His son, James, ran the business with assistance from his nephew, Walter J. Barth. When James died in 1923, Barth took a new partner, Ed Straub. They ran the operation until Prohibition and hard times forced them to close the doors.

In 1941, Barth moved into the old flour and feed store and started a restaurant, Barth's. His wife did much of the cooking. Their daughter Arleen married Palmer Krueger, and after World War II, the Barths hired Krueger to assist with food preparation and service. In 1950, a new barroom was added to the building and the old barroom was converted into what is now the main dining room. Barth retired in 1959 and the Kruegers became proprietors of this historic restaurant. Now their children are involved in the business. Son Peter is chef, having trained at Milwaukee Area Technical College. His brother, Thomas, is bar manager, and their sister, Mary Lou Grosser, is bookkeeper. All three are married and raising the sixth generation. The family works together, continuing more than 120 years in the restaurant business.

Through the years the restaurant has undergone remodeling and redecoration, but its roots are firmly planted in a tradition of fine dining. Its byword is "growing with the years; keeping the old hospitality." Two dining rooms house antique tableware, crewel work done by family members and 100-year-old paintings of local scenes. All of the food at Barth's is made in its kitchen, including all breads, muffins and desserts.

N58 W6194 Columbia Road
Cedarburg

SAUTEED CHICKEN LIVERS

2 pounds very fresh chicken livers
Flour
½ cup bacon fat
1 onion, chopped
1 cup sliced small mushrooms
Salt and freshly ground black pepper

1. Lightly flour the chicken livers.
2. Put the bacon fat in a skillet on high heat. Sauté the chicken livers with onion and mushrooms until livers are firm, about 5 minutes. Stir occasionally so that livers do not burn.
3. Season with salt and pepper. Divide among 6 appetizer plates and serve immediately.

It is important in this recipe to use bacon fat for sautéing the chicken livers because it will give the finished dish a good flavor. Be sure not to overcook the livers.

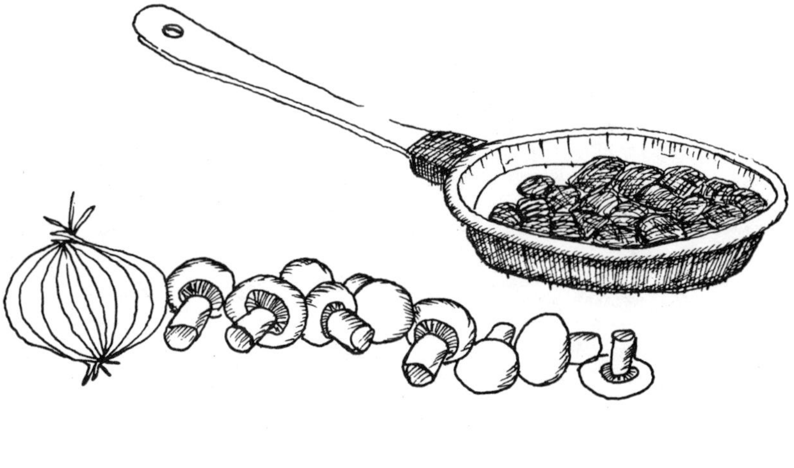

CHICKEN BROTH WITH PARSLEY DUMPLINGS

1 stewing hen, sectioned
1 gallon water
3 carrots
3 stalks celery
1 onion
8 black peppercorns
8 cloves
3 tablespoons salt
Parsley Dumplings

1. Place all the ingredients except the **Parsley Dumplings** in a large kettle or stockpot and bring to a boil. Reduce heat to simmer and cook 3 hours. Remove scum from the top of the stock occasionally.
2. Remove the stock from heat, strain and allow to cool at room temperature. Refrigerate, uncovered, until the fat congeals on top of stock. Remove the fat.
3. Strain the stock through a cheesecloth-lined sieve into a soup kettle and heat to serving temperature.
4. To serve, place 3 **Parsley Dumplings** in each of 6 soup bowls and cover with the hot chicken broth. Serve while hot.

Parsley Dumplings

1 cup flour (approximately)
1 teaspoon baking powder
½ teaspoon salt
2 eggs, beaten
⅔ cup milk
2 tablespoons vegetable oil
½ cup chopped parsley

1. Combine the flour, baking powder and salt in a mixing bowl. In another bowl, combine the eggs, milk and oil.
2. Preheat oven to 300°.
3. Add the parsley to the egg mixture and pour over the dry ingredients, stirring only enough to moisten dry ingredients. Additional flour may have to be added to make the mixture quite thick, like cookie dough.
4. Place a pan of hot water on the lowest shelf of the oven.
5. Drop batter by the ½ teaspoon onto an oiled baking sheet and bake on the second shelf in preheated oven 5 minutes. Remove the dumplings from the oven and cool.

Note: The broth can be made in advance and frozen if desired. The dumplings also can be made ahead and refrigerated until serving time.

Making the homemade broth as directed in the recipe will give the soup added flavor. When making the dumplings, be sure not to overmix the batter. Also, don't put the dumplings in the broth or they will break apart. It's best to put the dumplings in the soup bowls and ladle hot broth over them. They will be sufficiently heated by the hot broth; then serve the soup immediately.

TOSSED GARDEN SALAD
with Sour Cream Dressing

1 head iceberg lettuce, washed and chopped in 1" squares
2 carrots, peeled and shredded
8 radishes, sliced
1 cup shredded red cabbage
1 cup sliced cucumber
12 cherry tomatoes, stems removed
12 mushrooms, thinly sliced
Sour Cream Dressing

1. Place the lettuce in a large salad bowl. Add the carrot, radishes and red cabbage. Toss lightly. Place the cucumbers, cherry tomatoes and sliced mushrooms over the top of the salad.
2. Add **Sour Cream Dressing** gradually, tossing the salad, until it is dressed to desired taste. Divide among 6 salad plates or bowls and serve immediately.

Sour Cream Dressing

1 pint sour cream
½ teaspoon oregano
1 teaspoon salt
1 tablespoon vinegar
¼ teaspoon granulated onion
¼ teaspoon granulated garlic
⅛ teaspoon ground white pepper
Milk

Combine all ingredients except the milk in a mixing bowl. Add enough milk to make a creamy consistency.

Note: The dressing can be made ahead and refrigerated until serving time. It will keep well in the refrigerator for up to 2 weeks and can be used on other salads, too.

BEEF BURGUNDY

2½ pounds beef tenderloin tips
2 tablespoons clarified butter
1 tablespoon flour
Salt and freshly ground black pepper to taste
2 cloves garlic, crushed
1 quart dry red wine
Tied in a piece of cheesecloth:
1 stalk celery, cut up
1 sprig parsley
1 sprig fresh thyme
½ bay leaf
1 pound small white onions, peeled
3 tablespoons butter
Roux *(see next page)*
1 pound mushrooms, stems removed
1 tablespoon lemon juice
Chopped parsley for garnish

1. Sauté the beef tips in the clarified butter in a heavy-bottomed pan or casserole with a cover. Sprinkle the flour over the beef and cook until flour is browned, stirring.
2. Preheat oven to 350°.
3. Add the salt and pepper, garlic, wine and just enough water to cover meat (about 2 cups). Bring to a boil, add the cheesecloth bag of herbs (bouquet garni), cover the pan and braise in preheated oven 2 hours or until the meat is tender. Skim excess fat from the top of the beef. Remove the bouquet garni.
4. Brown the onions in 2 tablespoons butter in a sauté pan and stir into the beef over medium heat. Cook 15 minutes or until the onions are tender but still firm. Add the **Roux**, stirring, until mixture thickens.
5. Sauté the mushroom caps in 1 tablespoon butter, adding the lemon juice. Stir into the beef.
6. Sprinkle chopped parsley over the beef and serve immediately.

Note: This recipe can be made in advance through step 4. Use mushroom stems in other soups or cooking.

Roux

½ cup butter | *1 cup flour*

Heat the butter in a small saucepan until it sizzles. Add the flour all at once and stir to paste consistency using a wooden spoon. Cook 2 to 3 minutes, stirring constantly.

Do not omit the bouquet garni from this recipe. It will give the beef a special flavor.

SWEET AND SOUR RED CABBAGE

1 small onion, finely chopped
3 tablespoons butter
1 cup vinegar
⅓ cup sugar
¼ cup water
½ teaspoon ground cloves
1 tablespoon salt
1 teaspoon ground caraway seeds
1 small head red cabbage, cored and shredded
2½ tablespoons cornstarch, mixed with ¼ cup water

1. Sauté the onions in the butter until lightly browned. Set aside.
2. Put the vinegar, sugar, water, cloves, salt and caraway seeds in a saucepan and bring to a boil.
3. Add the cabbage and onion to the saucepan and simmer 45 minutes. The mixture should not cook dry.
4. Add the cornstarch mixture to the saucepan, stir and cook another 5 minutes. Serve immediately.

Note: This vegetable dish can be made in advance and reheated.

HERSHEY BAR TORTE

1½ cups finely crushed vanilla wafer crumbs
2 tablespoons melted butter
2 teaspoons unflavored gelatin
¼ cup milk
6 plain Hershey's chocolate candy bars, broken into pieces
2 cups miniature marshmallows
3 cups whipping cream, whipped stiff
Chocolate shavings for garnish

1. Prepare the crust by combining the wafer crumbs and melted butter. Pat into the bottom of a greased 9" x 13" pan. Set aside.
2. Combine the gelatin and milk in a small bowl and stir to dissolve gelatin. Pour into the top of a double boiler.
3. Put the double boiler over medium heat and add the candy bar pieces and marshmallows. Mix and cook over low heat until candy and marshmallows are melted. Remove from heat and cool 15 minutes.
4. Reserve one-fourth of the whipped cream; fold the remaining three-fourths into chocolate mixture. Pour the filling into the crust.
5. Spread the reserved whipped cream over the top of the filling and garnish with chocolate shavings. Refrigerate until serving time.

"A good chef must be imaginative, must be able to create and to stay one step ahead to be competitive," says chef Peter Krueger. "The hardest part about serving a meal in a restaurant is timing—putting it all together," he claims. "It requires coordination between the kitchen and the dining room, and extremely close coordination among all of the departments in the kitchen." He urges the home cook to do plenty of planning to guarantee successful entertaining. "Timing is essential when you're trying to serve a six-course meal. And it requires plenty of thought and as much advance preparation as possible."

le bistro

Dinner for Four

Stuffed Mushroom Appetizer

Crayfish Soup

Salade Mikado

Sirloin Steak in Bleu Cheese Sauce

Green Beans Almondine

Apple Soufflé

Wine:

Châteauneuf-du-Pape, 1974

The Marcus Corporation, Proprietor
Gaspar Stantic, Executive Chef

LE BISTRO

Le Bistro, located in the Marc Plaza Hotel, featues an extensive Continental menu with accents on French classic and nouvelle cuisines. Many of the dishes are prepared tableside and are complemented by wines from a cellar that boasts 250 different varieties. In addition, the luncheon menu features a different international buffet every few weeks, offering some of Executive Chef Gaspar Stantic's favorite dishes, many of which are from Hungary.

Chef Stantic is a native of Yugoslavia and a graduate of the Vocational Training School for Hotels and Restaurants in Belgrade, Yugoslavia. He received his master training in Vienna and has a cooking career that spans twenty years. Fluent in Hungarian, Serbo-Croation, German, Finnish, French and English, Stantic has held positions as sous chef and executive chef for first-class hotels and restaurants in Morocco, Amsterdam, Munich, Hong Kong, Kuwait and Hungary, including Hong Kong's prestigious Peninsula Hotel, as well as the Royal Caribbean Cruise Line. In America, before joining the Marcus Corporation and Le Bistro, Stantic was executive sous chef at the Omni International Hotel in Atlanta, Georgia.

Chef Stantic has been honored by the Chaîne des Rôtisseurs society. As a member of the Yugoslavian Olympic Culinary Team, he was given the *Bilten,* the highest medal for international cooking awarded by the Yugoslavian government. He has also won awards in 1980 at Knoxville's Dogwood Culinary Art Salon, the National Restaurant Assocation's tenth National Culinary Salon competition and the Grant Buffet Award for best overall display in the 1980 Culinary Arts show sponsored by the Professional Chefs and Cooks Association of Milwaukee.

Le Bistro was opened in 1974, and after one year in operation it won the distinquished *Holiday* Award, which it has continued to earn every year since. It provides tasteful, intimate dining, with richly-upholstered furnishings, crystal and formally-attired waiters.

509 West Wisconsin Avenue

STUFFED MUSHROOM APPETIZER

1 cup flaked crab meat
¼ cup fresh bread crumbs
2 tablespoons Dijon mustard
2 tablespoons dry white wine
¼ cup **Mornay Sauce**
Salt and freshly ground black pepper to taste
12 large mushroom caps, cleaned
1 cup Hollandaise Sauce (see index)

1. Preheat oven to 350°.
2. Combine the crab, bread crumbs, mustard, wine and **Mornay Sauce** in a mixing bowl. Mix gently but thoroughly.
3. Season to taste with salt and pepper. Stuff mushroom caps with the mixture. Place 3 stuffed mushroom caps in each of 4 small gratin dishes.
4. Bake the gratin dishes 15 minutes, or until the mushrooms are soft, in preheated oven. Remove and pour ¼ cup Hollandaise Sauce over each gratin dish.
5. Place under hot broiler to brown slightly. Serve immediately.

Mornay Sauce

3 egg yolks, lightly beaten
2 tablespoons cream
2 cups WHITE SAUCE (see next page)
2 tablespoons butter
2 tablespoons grated Parmesan cheese
2 tablespoons grated Swiss cheese

1. Mix the egg yolks with the cream in a small bowl.
2. Place the *WHITE SAUCE* in a saucepan to heat. Add the yolks and cream and cook, stirring constantly, until the sauce just reaches the boiling point.
3. Add the butter and both cheeses and stir to combine.

WHITE SAUCE

2 tablespoons butter
2 tablespoons flour
2 cups milk
¼ teaspoon white pepper
½ teaspoon salt

1. Melt the butter over medium-low heat and blend in the flour. Cook, stirring constantly, about 10 minutes. Do not allow to brown.
2. Heat the milk almost to scalding in a separate pan. Pour half into the hot roux and blend until smooth, then blend in the remaining half.
3. Add the white pepper and salt and simmer carefully for 15 minutes, never allowing to boil.

Note: The appetizer can be made in advance through step 3. White Sauce, Mornay Sauce and Hollandaise can be made in advance. Take care when reheating Hollandaise that the butter does not separate from the sauce. Extra Mornay Sauce can be covered and refrigerated. Reheat on low heat and serve with cooked vegetables.

CRAYFISH SOUP

1 rib celery, coarsely chopped
¼ cup chopped onion
¼ cup chopped carrot
1 teaspoon crushed fresh garlic
1 teaspoon chopped shallot
2 tablespoons butter
2 tablespoons flour
2 tablespoons tomato paste
2 cups Fish Stock (see index)
½ cup dry white wine
1 teaspoon dried tarragon
1 teaspoon chopped parsley
½ pound frozen crayfish meat, thawed
¼ cup heavy cream
Salt and freshly ground white pepper to taste

1. Sauté the celery, onion, carrot, garlic and shallot in butter in a soup kettle until the vegetables are soft.
2. Add the flour, stirring into the butter. Add the tomato paste, Fish Stock and wine, stirring well. Add the tarragon and parsley and simmer 30 minutes.
3. Purée the mixture in a blender or food processor until creamy in texture. Strain back into the soup kettle.
4. Add the crayfish. Simmer 15 minutes, stirring occasionally. Add the cream and season to taste. Serve immediately.

Note: The soup can be made in advance through step 3. Add the fish and heat shortly before serving.

Don't allow the crayfish meat to overcook in the soup.

SALADE MIKADO

2 avocados
12 mushrooms, thinly sliced
1 cup peeled, diced and seeded tomato
1 ounce truffle, julienned (optional)
Vinaigrette Dressing

1. Halve the avocados, remove the pits and peel. Rinse in cold water to prevent discoloration and slice thinly. Arrange one-fourth of the avocado slices in a semi-circle on one side of each salad plate.
2. Arrange one-fourth of the mushroom slices on the other side of each plate.
3. Place the tomatoes down the centers of the plates.
4. Sprinkle one-fourth of the truffle (optional) over each salad. Cover with plastic wrap and chill.
5. Drizzle **Vinaigrette Dressing** over the salads and serve immediately.

Vinaigrette Dressing

2 tablespoons vinegar
½ teaspoon salt
¼ teaspoon freshly ground black pepper
½ cup olive or salad oil

1. Mix the vinegar and salt in a bowl and let stand 1 minute. Add the pepper and slowly whisk in the oil.
2. Taste and add more salt if necessary. Store in a jar with a lid and shake well before serving.

Note: The salad dressing must be made in advance. Leftover dressing can be kept covered and refrigerated to use on other salads. The salads can be made in advance through step 4 about 2 or 3 hours in advance of serving.

Truffle in the salad is a nice touch, but not necessary if one doesn't want to go to the expense.

SIRLOIN STEAK
in Bleu Cheese Sauce

1 ounce bleu cheese
1 cup heavy cream
1 tablespoon chopped shallots
2 tablespoons dry white wine
¼ cup cooking oil
4 (8-ounce) strip loin steaks
Salt and freshly ground black pepper to taste

1. Combine the bleu cheese, cream and shallots in a saucepan. Stir and simmer slowly to reduce in volume.
2. Add the wine and cook, reducing the sauce until slightly thickened. Set aside.
3. Brush the oil on the steaks and broil to desired doneness.
4. Place the steaks on hot plates. Bring the sauce to a simmer, season to taste with salt and pepper and ladle over the steaks. Serve immediately.

Note: This recipe can be made in advance through step 2.

GREEN BEANS ALMONDINE

1 pound green beans
2 tablespoons butter
⅓ cup blanched slivered almonds
Salt
Freshly ground black pepper

1. Wash the green beans and remove ends and strings. Leave whole or cut in diagonal strips. Steam, covered, in a steamer basket over 1″ rapidly boiling water until just tender, but still crunchy—10 to 15 minutes. Drain and set aside.
2. Heat the butter in a large skillet and add the almonds. Cook until lightly browned. Add the beans to the skillet and cook to reheat. Add salt and pepper to taste and serve immediately.

Note: This recipe can be made in advance through step 1.

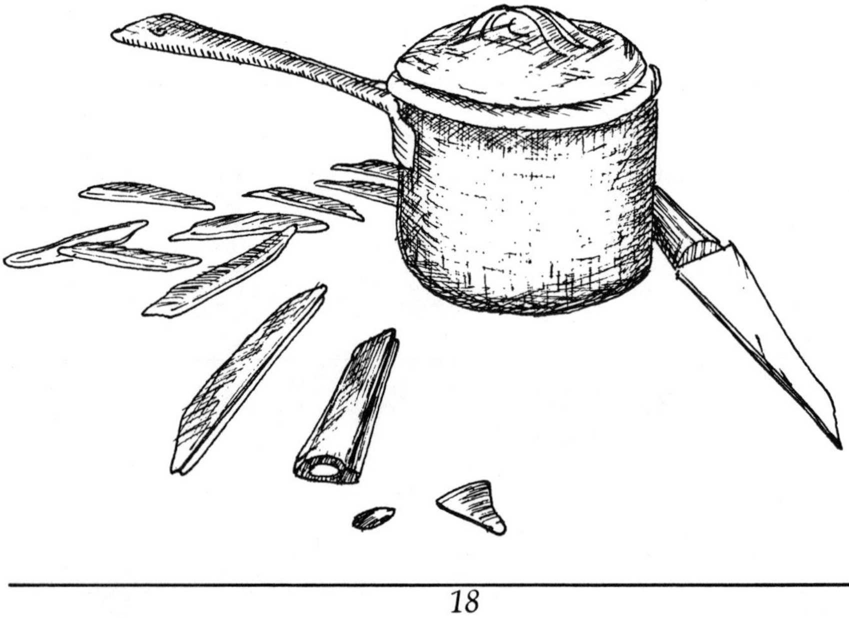

APPLE SOUFFLE

1 cup milk
1 vanilla bean
5½ tablespoons sugar
¼ cup flour
1½ tablespoons butter
3 tablespoons Calvados
3 eggs, separated
2 apples, peeled, cut into very thin slices
Powdered sugar

1. Preheat oven to 350°.
2. Reserve 3 tablespoons milk. Place the remainder with the vanilla bean in a saucepan and bring to a boil. Remove from heat and set aside.
3. Mix 4 tablespoons sugar, the flour and the reserved 3 tablespoons milk in a mixing bowl and stir with a spatula to combine. While stirring, gradually add half the hot milk. Mix well. Discard the vanilla bean and add the remaining hot milk, beating constantly. Pour back into the saucepan and bring to a boil. Boil 2 minutes.
4. Remove from heat and stir in the butter and 1½ tablespoons Calvados. Cover and allow to cool slightly. While still warm, add the egg yolks and mix well, quickly, so that the eggs are well combined. Cool.
5. Beat the egg whites until frothy. Add the remaining 1½ tablespoons sugar and beat until very stiff. Fold the whites into the batter.
6. Pour one-third of the batter into a buttered and sugared 8″ soufflé dish. Place a layer of apple slices over the batter. Add another third of the batter and a layer of apple. Top with the remaining batter and apple. Sprinkle with powdered sugar.
7. Bake in preheated oven 25 minutes. Just before serving, heat the remaining 1½ tablespoons Calvados in a saucepan and ignite. Pour the flaming liqueur over the soufflé and serve immediately.

The Black Kettle

Dinner for Four

Escargot Appetizer

Baked Onion Soup

Fresh Mushroom Salad

Pepper Steak

Hot Rum Sundae

Wine:

St.-Emilion

Dorothy Edwards, Proprietor
Randy Schmidt, Chef

THE BLACK KETTLE

The Black Kettle got its start in Milwaukee in 1963 when Dorothy Edwards, previously a food buyer for Marquette University, bought the small restaurant. She looked upon the business as a big challenge and it took her two and a half years to get the restaurant "on its feet." Word of mouth was, and still is, one of the best methods of advertising for this cozy Williamsburg-style restaurant. Regarded as very much of a hideaway in the early years, the Black Kettle now caters to a diverse clientele.

From the start Mrs. Edwards baked all of the breads and desserts, and made all of the salad dressings and sauces. That still happens, but now a trained crew does the cooking. "We have pride in our food. That's why we make it all here," she said.

The effort at this restaurant is to make people feel as comfortable and relaxed as if they were in their own homes. "Our motto is to serve good food, provide good service and to know that the customer is always right," she adds.

There are three sons: Paul, who has worked in the restaurant and now assists in managing it; John, who tends bar while going to school; and Peter, who is too young to be an active part in the business now.

A good chef loves food and has a feel for it, in Mrs. Edwards's estimation. Most home kitchens are not designed for the hard work of cooking, thus making it more difficult to cook at home. Mrs. Edwards tests and perfects recipes once or twice a week in a small "test kitchen" within the restaurant kitchen.

8660 North 107th Street

ESCARGOT APPETIZER

1¼ cups butter
2 teaspoons finely chopped shallots
2 cloves garlic, crushed
1 teaspoon chopped parsley
1 teaspoon chopped chives
Salt and ground white pepper to taste
20 canned snails with shells
2 tablespoons dry white wine
Fine bread crumbs
Fresh french bread, sliced

1. Preheat oven to 450°.
2. Cream the butter using a mixer. Blend in the shallots, garlic, parsley, chives, salt and pepper.
3. Place ½ teaspoon seasoned butter in the bottom of each snail shell. Place 1 snail on top of the butter in each shell and cover with the remaining butter.
4. Put the white wine in the bottom of a pan large enough to hold all the snails. Arrange the snails in the pan and sprinkle with bread crumbs.
5. Bake in preheated oven until the bread crumbs are browned.
6. Divide the snails among 4 appetizer plates and serve immediately with french bread for sopping up butter.

Note: This appetizer can be prepared in advance through step 4.

It is important not to omit the shallots from this recipe. They give the appetizer a special flavor.

BAKED ONION SOUP

4 onions, thinly sliced
1 tablespoon butter
1 tablespoon flour
1 quart Beef Stock (see index) or bouillon
4 thin slices french bread, toasted
½ pound Swiss cheese, grated
¼ pound Parmesan cheese, grated

1. Sauté the onions in butter in a sauté pan slowly until tender and golden brown, stirring constantly, about 20 minutes. Stir in the flour, cooking 2 minutes.
2. Preheat broiler.
3. Add the stock or bouillon to the onions and cook 20 minutes. Pour the soup into 4 (8-ounce) soup crocks. Top each crock with 1 slice toasted french bread.
4. Combine the Swiss and Parmesan cheeses and sprinkle over the toast, dividing evenly among the crocks. Put the crocks on a cookie sheet and place under the hot broiler until the cheese melts and browns. Serve immediately.

Note: The soup can be prepared in advance, but it should be hot when cheese is melted under the broiler just before serving.

FRESH MUSHROOM SALAD

1 pound mushrooms, cleaned, dried and thinly sliced
1 cup vegetable oil
¼ cup lemon juice
1 teaspoon salt
½ teaspoon garlic salt
Lettuce

1. Place the mushrooms in a bowl.
2. Put the oil, lemon juice, salt and garlic salt in a jar with a lid. Cover and shake to combine ingredients.
3. Pour over the mushrooms and toss gently to coat. Cover and refrigerate, allowing the mushrooms to marinate in the dressing at least 30 minutes.
4. Line 4 salad plates or bowls with lettuce and divide the mushroom mixture among them. Serve immediately.

Be sure to marinate the mushrooms for maximum flavor. Don't marinate more than two hours.

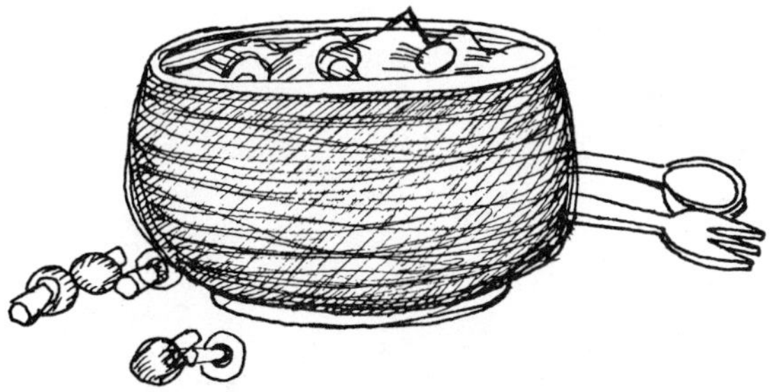

PEPPER STEAK

4 tablespoons butter
4 cloves garlic, slivered
1 pound beef tenderloin, cut 1/4" by 2"
2 1/4 teaspoons salt
1 teaspoon oregano
1/2 teaspoon freshly ground black pepper
1/4 cup sherry or sauterne
1 (8-ounce) can tomato sauce
1/4 cup vegetable oil
4 large green peppers, diced 1 1/2"
1/2 pound mushrooms, sliced
2 medium-sized tomatoes, cored and quartered

1. Melt the butter in a sauté pan over medium heat. Sauté 3 slivered garlic cloves 1 minute, stirring constantly.
2. Add the beef, cooking 2 to 3 minutes on each side or until the meat browns, over high heat. Season with 1 1/4 teaspoons salt, 1/2 teaspoon oregano and 1/4 teaspoon pepper. Add the wine and tomato sauce. Cover the pan and steam about 5 minutes, stirring occasionally.
3. Put the vegetable oil in another sauté pan and heat over medium heat. Add the green peppers, mushrooms and remaining clove of garlic and cook 5 minutes, stirring occasionally. Season with the remaining salt, pepper and oregano. Cover and steam 5 minutes, stirring occasionally. (The vegetables should be crisp-tender and the peppers should not lose their bright green color).
5. Add the tomatoes and cook until just warm, but still firm.
6. Combine the meat and vegetable mixtures and serve at once. This entrée may be served over hot rice if desired.

Note: All of the ingredients for this recipe should be measured and prepared in advance, but the cooking should not occur until just before serving time.

Be sure not to overcook the vegetables.

HOT RUM SUNDAE

4 large scoops vanilla ice cream
1 small can sliced pears, drained
Rum Sauce

Place 1 scoop vanilla ice cream in each of 4 dessert bowls. Divide the pears among the bowls. Top with **Rum Sauce** and serve immediately.

Rum Sauce

½ cup butter
1 cup sugar
¼ cup light rum
Dash of ground cinnamon

Place all ingredients in a saucepan and bring to a boil. Boil 2 minutes. Remove from the heat and cool. Serve as directed.

Note: The sauce should be prepared in advance and kept at room temperature until serving time. Extra sauce can be stored in a jar in the refrigerator.

The pears add a lot to this recipe. Don't shy away from them just because they are canned–they do add a lot to this dessert.

Boder's on-the-river

Dinner for Four

Strawberry Collins

Zwiebelkuchen

Chicken Egg Drop Soup

Fresh Marinated Tomato Salad

Baked Stuffed Rainbow Trout

Baked Zucchini Squash

Boder's Corn Fritters

Blueberry Muffins

Mocha Fudge Ice Cream Torte

Wine:

With the Zwiebelkuchen–Geyser Peak Johannisberg Riesling
With the Trout–Geyser Peak Chardonnay

Jack and Dolly Boder, Fred and Mary Krautkramer,
John and Nancy Walch, and Jean Fisher, Proprietors
John Walch, Jr., Chef

BODER'S ON THE RIVER

Boder's-on-the-River in Mequon is dedicated to its motto: "Good food is good health." Its reputation has been built on good-quality food, and it has received several awards testifying to its excellence. All of its specialties, including the famous Corn Fritters and popular Blueberry and Cherry Muffins, are made on the premises. A delicious fresh fruit tray, which accompanies every order at Boder's, is served year-round.

Since its founding in 1929, Boder's has been a family-operated restaurant. John and Frieda Boder converted an 1840 homestead situated near the Milwaukee River which had been used as a summer camp for underprivileged children. Frieda did all of the cooking in those days, while husband John managed the dining room.

Jack and Dolly Boder bought the restaurant from Jack's parents in 1954, continuing the family tradition. They had gathered the necessary expertise and knowledge to take charge by working part-time at the restaurant. Eventually three daughters and two sons-in-law joined the business. John Walch, Jr. is head chef and kitchen manager while Fred Krautkramer is in charge of the dining room and bar.

Daughter Nancy Walch is the head supervisor in the kitchen and her sister, Mary Krautkramer, is the dining room hostess. Both also manage the gift room and tend the many gardens on the premises which provide fresh flowers for the tables in the four dining rooms. Their sister, Jean Fisher, is the business manager and handles all of the public relations and advertising for the restaurant.

Although Jack and Dolly Boder are semi-retired, they still help wherever needed. Having worked as chef after her mother-in-law, Dolly believes that a good chef must love to cook and want to improvise. In addition, he or she must be interested in all parts of the restaurant, understanding the dining room as well as the kitchen.

11919 North River Road 43W
Mequon

STRAWBERRY COLLINS

12 to 16 large ice cubes
24 strawberries
½ cup lemon juice
18 to 24 ounces 7-Up
¼ cup powdered sugar

1. Hull 20 strawberries, reserving 4 unhulled as garnish.
2. Put 4 large ice cubes in a blender. Add 10 hulled strawberries, 2 ounces lemon juice, 6 ounces 7-Up and 2 tablespoons powdered sugar. Blend 30 seconds or until well mixed.
3. Pour into 2 tall glasses and add more ice and 7-Up to fill the glasses. Garnish each with 1 unhulled strawberry.
4. Make 2 more drinks in the same manner.

It is best to use fresh strawberries in this recipe, but when they are not available, frozen sweetened strawberries could be used. If the latter is used, reduce the amount of powdered sugar to taste.

Although Boder's serves many mixed cocktails, non-alcoholic cocktails are popular at the restaurant, too. For an alcoholic drink, add 1 jigger gin, vodka or rum to each drink.

ZWIEBELKUCHEN

1 cup all-purpose flour
¾ teaspoon salt
Dash of sugar
¼ pound butter, room temperature
2 tablespoons milk
6 slices bacon, cut into small pieces
3 cups chopped onion
2 eggs, beaten
2 egg yolks, beaten
¾ cup sour cream
⅛ teaspoon ground black pepper
1 teaspoon chopped chives
¼ teaspoon caraway seeds

1. Sift the flour, ¼ teaspoon salt and sugar into a bowl. Cut in the butter. Add the milk, mixing with a fork to moisten flour. Shape into a ball, wrap in plastic and chill 1 hour.
2. Preheat to 350°.
3. Roll the pastry between sheets of wax paper and then fit into a 9″ pie plate. Prick the crust lightly. Bake in preheated oven 10 minutes or until lightly browned. Cool.
4. Preheat oven to 375°.
5. Fry the bacon until crisp; remove from the pan. Sauté the onion in the bacon fat until soft. Drain off fat.
6. Place the bacon in a bowl and add the eggs, egg yolks, sour cream, ½ teaspoon salt, pepper and chives. Beat lightly; add the sautéed onions. Pour into the baked crust. Sprinkle with caraway seeds.
7. Bake in preheated oven 30 to 35 minutes. Cut into wedges to serve.

Note: The onion pie can be completely made in advance, baked and frozen. To serve, allow it to thaw, covered, and warm in a preheated 300° oven 15 to 20 minutes. It will serve more than 4 as an appetizer. The recipe cannot be reduced without affecting the quality. The pie also can be cut into 36 to 40 bite-size pieces and served as an appetizer to a large group of people.

It is important to brown the onions, but not to overcook them. The onion pie is much like a quiche, but because it does not contain a custard, the texture is not the same.

CHICKEN EGG DROP SOUP

1 quart Chicken Stock (see index)
3 tablespoons grated carrot
1/8 teaspoon freshly ground black pepper
Salt
1 egg
3 tablespoons flour
1/4 cup water
1/4 teaspoon baking powder
Freshly chopped parsley for garnish

1. Pour the Chicken Stock into a soup kettle and add the carrot, black pepper and salt to taste. Heat.
2. Beat the egg in a small bowl. Add 1/8 teaspoon salt, flour, water and baking powder. Stir until smooth.
3. Bring the soup to a boil. Pour the egg mixture from the end of a spoon into the boiling soup. Cook 2 to 3 minutes.
4. Pour the soup into bowls and garnish with chopped parsley.

Note: The soup can be made ahead through step 1, but the egg mixture should be stirred in just before serving or it will settle to the bottom of the soup and is likely to burn when reheated.

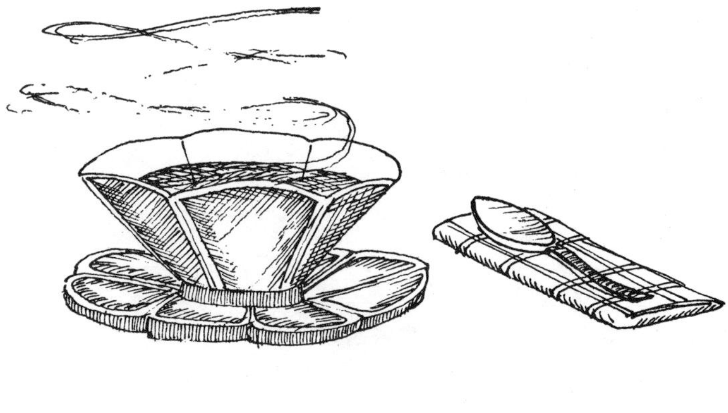

FRESH MARINATED TOMATO SALAD

6 medium-size ripe tomatoes, cut into large bite-size pieces (approximately 3 cups)
1 cup finely chopped celery
½ cup finely chopped green pepper
1 tablespoon whole mustard seed
1½ teaspoons salt
½ cup sugar
½ cup vinegar
4 large leaves fresh lettuce

1. Combine all ingredients except the lettuce in a large bowl and mix well. Cover and refrigerate at least 24 hours.
2. Place 1 lettuce leaf in the bottom of each of 4 salad bowls and divide the salad mixture among the bowls, being sure to spoon some of the liquid over the tomatoes. Serve immediately.

This salad will keep in the refrigerator for up to 5 or 6 days. It is essential to allow time for the tomatoes to marinate in the dressing.

BAKED STUFFED RAINBOW TROUT

12 slices white bread, broken into small pieces
2 tablespoons chopped parsley
1 teaspoon grated onion
Salt
1 teaspoon Accent
¾ cup milk
⅓ cup dry sauterne
¼ pound plus 2 tablespoons butter, melted
1 egg
4 rainbow trout, boned, completely thawed if frozen
Flour
Paprika
4 lemon wedges
Tartar sauce (optional)

1. Place the bread pieces, parsley, onion, 2 teaspoons salt and Accent in a mixing bowl. Mix together. Add the milk, wine, all but 2 tablespoons of the butter and the egg. Mix well with an electric mixer on low speed. Do not overmix.
2. Preheat oven to 400°.
3. Stuff each trout with dressing. Flour lightly and sprinkle with salt, remaining butter and paprika.
4. Place the stuffed trout on a well-buttered pan and bake in preheated oven about 20 minutes or until golden brown and the flesh flakes.
5. Serve the trout with lemon wedges, and tartar sauce if desired.

It is important not to overmix the stuffing. The fish can be stuffed early in the day, but should not be cooked until just prior to serving.

BAKED ZUCCHINI SQUASH

4 medium-size zucchini, sliced in half lengthwise
4 tablespoons melted butter
Salt
Soda cracker crumbs, finely crushed
Paprika

1. Preheat oven to 350°.
2. Place the zucchini in a baking pan, cut side up. Brush with 2 tablespoons melted butter and salt lightly.
3. Place the remaining butter in a skillet and brown the cracker crumbs over very low heat.
4. Sprinkle the crumbs over the zucchini. Sprinkle paprika over the crumbs.
5. Bake in preheated oven about 15 minutes or until the squash is tender when pierced with a fork or sharp knife.

Note: This recipe can be prepared in advance through step 4.

Be sure not to overbake the squash or it will become mushy.

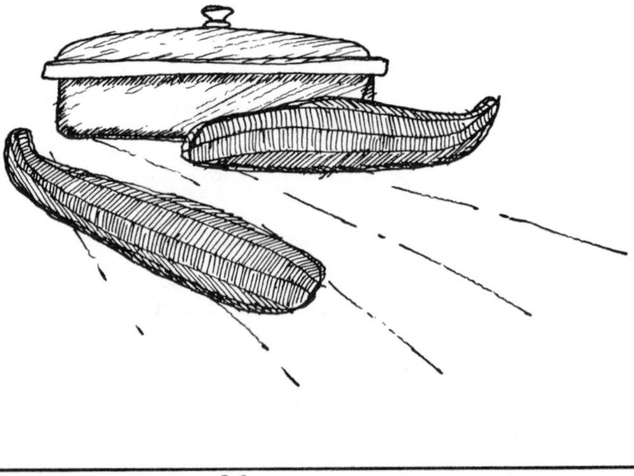

BODER'S CORN FRITTERS

1 cup flour
½ teaspoon salt
1 tablespoon baking powder
1½ teaspoons corn oil
1 teaspoon vinegar
½ cup milk
2 eggs, separated
½ cup whole kernel corn, drained
Shortening for frying
Powdered sugar
Maple syrup

1. Sift the dry ingredients and place in a bowl. Add the corn oil, vinegar, milk, egg yolks and corn. Mix well. The mixture should be moist, not dry.
2. Beat the egg whites until stiff, then fold into the corn mixture.
3. Preheat oven to 325°.
4. Fill a deep skillet with shortening and heat to 350°.
5. Drop large spoonfuls of batter into the hot shortening, deep-frying until golden brown. Place the browned fritters on empty muffin tins.
6. Bake in preheated oven 10 minutes. Remove from the tins and sprinkle the fritters with powdered sugar. Serve with maple syrup.

Note: Corn Fritters can be made in advance, frozen, thawed and reheated as directed in step 6. Place them on a muffin tin to reheat so that excess shortening accumulates in the tin, not in the fritter.

It is essential that the shortening be fresh and heated to the right temperature before the fritter batter is added. An electric skillet can be used for cooking the fritters. By baking them in the oven for 10 minutes, the excess shortening is baked out of the fritters so they are not greasy.

Corn fritters accompany every order at Boder's.

BLUEBERRY MUFFINS

2 cups sifted flour
4 teaspoons baking powder
¾ cup sugar
1 teaspoon salt
1 cup fresh, frozen or canned blueberries (drained if canned)
2 eggs
½ cup melted butter
1 cup milk
Cinnamon and Sugar Topping

1. Put paper muffin cup liners in 12 to 14 muffin cups. Preheat oven to 400°.
2. Sift all dry ingredients together in a large bowl.
3. Add the blueberries and mix until well coated. (It is not necessary to thaw frozen blueberries.)
4. Beat the eggs well in a small bowl. Add the melted butter and milk. Quickly stir the liquid mixture into the dry mixture. Do not overmix as overblending will cause a tough texture.
5. Fill muffin cups three-fourths full and sprinkle with **Cinnamon and Sugar Topping.**
6. Bake in preheated oven 20 minutes or until brown.

Use only butter in this recipe; do not substitute margarine or shortening. Pitted tart cherries may be substituted for the blueberries.

Cinnamon and Sugar Topping

⅛ teaspoon ground cinnamon
½ cup sugar

Mix ingredients together and use as directed.

Note: The muffins can be baked in advance and frozen. To reheat, thaw and warm in the oven as you would dinner rolls.

Like Corn Fritters, Blueberry Muffins accompany every order at Boder's.

MOCHA FUDGE ICE CREAM TORTE

Graham Cracker Crust
1½ quarts coffee ice cream
Chocolate fudge topping
Chopped salted pecans

1. Cover the bottom of a 9″ by 13″ by 2″ pan with **Graham Cracker Crust.**
2. Slightly soften the ice cream and spread it evenly over the crust, using a spoon or knife. Cover and freeze overnight.
3. Frost with cold fudge topping and sprinkle with pecans. Cover and freeze until serving time.

Note: This recipe will serve more than 4. Leftover dessert keeps well, covered tightly, in the freezer.

Be sure to refreeze the ice cream before adding the fudge topping and completely cover the ice cream with the topping.

Graham Cracker Crust

2 cups graham cracker crumbs
¼ cup sugar
¼ pound butter, melted

Mix all ingredients together.

BOULEVARD INN

Dinner for Six

Chopped Chicken Liver Pâté

Baked French Onion Soup

Terrence Salad with Dijon Mustard Vinaigrette

Baked Breast of Chicken Kiev with Wild Rice Dressing

Stir-Fried Fresh Vegetable Medley in Garlic Butter

Pashka with Raspberry Melba Sauce

Wine:

Hoffman Mountain Ranch Chenin Blanc, 1979
or
Robert Mondavi Chenin Blanc, 1980
or
Yverdon Chenin Blanc, 1979

Mark, Gary, Werner and Joan Strothmann, Owners
Mark Strothmann, General Manager
Dennis Kuhfuss, Chef

BOULEVARD INN

The Boulevard Inn has a long history in Milwaukee, dating from 1910, but it wasn't until 1946 that a restaurant family headed by Albert Gaulke bought the restaurant. Previously he had run a downtown Milwaukee coffee shop. Today the Boulevard Inn is one of Milwaukee's finest dining establishments. Gaulke's grandson, Mark Strothmann, is general manager and primarily responsible for the day-to-day running of the business, in addition to determining the changing trends in dining. He and his family are the current owners of the restaurant.

"I think we are unique," he says. "My philosophy is to make everything from scratch on the premises, and that includes our salad dressings, our breads and all of our baking. If we bought from the same purveyors as our competitors, there would be less difference between us. That's why we do all of our cooking. We buy our meats from the most expensive retailer in town, and our ducks are purchased fresh, never frozen.

"We use a lot of butter in cooking and the emphasis is always on fresh, quality ingredients," says Strothman. Although he enjoys cooking, Strothmann seeks chefs who are creative and inventive, and at the same time open to suggestion and new ways. "I like to run a peaceful operation with no intimidation. Some chefs can be intimidating," he adds. "I like a good cooking fundamentalist who knows soups and sauces and Kuhfuss is that man. We found him in Colorado, and he's been with us for eight years."

4700 W. Lloyd St.

CHOPPED CHICKEN LIVER PATE

2 pounds chicken livers
½ medium-size yellow onion, chopped
2 beef bouillon cubes
2 to 3 ounces cream cheese, softened
1 teaspoon Worcestershire sauce
1 teaspoon garlic powder
Salt to taste
6 crisp green lettuce leaves
2 hard-cooked egg yolks, sieved
2 kosher garlic dill pickles, thinly sliced lengthwise
1 sweet red onion, peeled and cut into 6 thin slices
Crackers of your choice

1. Place the chicken livers, chopped yellow onion and beef bouillon in a saucepan and add just enough water to cover. Boil until the livers are cooked through, 15 to 20 minutes.
2. Remove the livers and onion from the liquid and place in the work bowl of a food processor fitted with a steel blade. Process to grind the livers and onion. Add the cream cheese, Worcestershire sauce and garlic powder and process to a very smooth consistency. Taste and add salt if necessary. Chill.
3. Line 6 chilled plates with lettuce. Using an ice cream scoop, place a scoop of pâté on each plate over the lettuce. Sprinkle with sieved egg yolk. Garnish each plate with pickle slices, a red onion slice and crackers.

Note: The pâté can be made 4 to 5 days in advance.

The trick to this recipe is in getting the livers blended really smooth. Cream cheese is the secret. I experimented with sour cream and mayonnaise before I found that cream cheese provided what I was looking for.

BAKED FRENCH ONION SOUP

2 quarts Beef Stock (see index)
1 bay leaf
½ teaspoon thyme
4 to 5 beef bouillon cubes
2 large onions, peeled, sliced and separated into rings
Roux
6 slices toasted rye bread
1½ cups grated Swiss cheese
½ cup grated Parmesan cheese

1. Put the Beef Stock, bay leaf, thyme, bouillon cubes and onion slices in a large pot. Bring to a boil and cook until the onions are soft, about 30 minutes. Remove the bay leaf.
2. Preheat oven to 400°.
3. Whisk **Roux** into the soup to thicken to desired consistency.
4. Divide the soup into 6 crocks. Place a slice of rye toast on top of each bowl of soup, cutting the toast to fit the bowl if necessary. Sprinkle ¼ cup grated Swiss cheese on top of the toast in each bowl. Sprinkle grated Parmesan over the Swiss cheese.
5. Bake in preheated oven 5 to 10 minutes, or until the cheese melts and browns slightly.

Roux

¼ pound butter
½ cup flour

Melt the butter in a saucepan over medium-high heat. When bubbling, add the flour, stirring with a wooden spoon. Cook 2 to 3 minutes, stirring constantly, until the mixture is like paste. Remove from heat.

Note: The recipe can be made in advance through step 4.

This is not the ordinary thin-stock French onion soup, but a thick, hearty-style potage. It is very important to thicken by adding the roux gradually. I spent many years searching for an acceptable Baked French Onion recipe. I ate onion soup all over the world before finding this one in New Orleans.

TERRENCE SALAD
with Dijon Vinaigrette Dressing

6 crisp lettuce leaves
3 large tomatoes, sliced 1/4"
1 large sweet red onion, peeled and cut into 12 (1/8") slices
Vinaigrette Dressing

1. Line 6 chilled flat plates with lettuce leaves. For each salad, place 1 slice tomato on the lettuce, three-fourths covered by 1 slice onion. Top with another tomato slice, three-fourths covered by another onion slice. Top with another tomato slice.
2. Sparingly drizzle dressing over each salad and serve immediately.

Vinaigrette Dressing

1/4 cup champagne wine vinegar
3/4 cup good-quality salad oil
1/4 teaspoon sea salt, ground in mortar with pestle
1/4 cup Dijon mustard

Put the vinegar in the work bowl of a food processor fitted with a steel blade. With the machine running, slowly add the oil in a thin stream until all is absorbed. With the machine still running, add the salt and mustard.

This is really an easy salad and dressing, especially if the dressing is made in a food processor. If not made in a food processor, take care to add the oil very gradually.

BAKED BREAST OF CHICKEN KIEV
with Wild Rice Dressing

6 (12-ounce) whole chicken breasts, skinned and boned
Flavored Butter
Flour
1 egg, beaten with 1 cup milk
2 cups dry bread crumbs
Wild Rice Dressing
Sauce *(see second page following)*

1. Pound the chicken breasts with a mallet until thin.
2. Place ½ cup **Flavored Butter** over the center of each chicken breast. Wrap the chicken breasts as tightly as possible around the butter, tucking in the ends of the meat so that no butter is visible.
3. Preheat oven to 450°.
4. Roll the filled chicken breasts in flour and dip in the egg wash, then roll in the bread crumbs. Return to the egg wash and back to the bread crumbs once more, coating well.
5. Brown the chicken breasts lightly in a deep-fryer heated to 375°. Remove and place in a baking pan. Cover and bake in preheated oven 30 minutes.
6. Put ½ cup hot **Wild Rice Dressing** on each plate and top with a chicken breast. Cover with hot **Sauce**. Serve immediately with the remaining sauce at table.

Note: The chicken can be made in advance through step 4. The Flavored Butter can be made in advance and frozen. The sauce can be made in advance and reheated over low heat. The rice, also, may be made in advance. Reheat it by placing in a colander inside a pot and steaming it.

Flavored Butter

1 pound butter, softened
2 tablespoons granulated garlic
1½ teaspoons Worcestershire sauce
½ teaspoon Tabasco sauce
2 teaspoons freshly ground white pepper
1 tablespoon chopped parsley
¼ cup dry white wine
1 tablespoon Lawry's seasoned salt

Put the ingredients in a mixing bowl or food processor and whip until well blended. Divide the mixture into 6 equal portions, forming each into a ball. Freeze before using to fill the chicken breasts.

Wild Rice Dressing

½ pound brown rice
½ cup salad oil
4 chicken bouillon cubes
1 (6-ounce) package Uncle Ben's Wild Rice Mix
1 teaspoon poultry seasoning

1. Mix the brown rice with the oil and sauté until the rice is slightly browned. Drain off any excess oil.
2. Preheat oven to 350°.
3. Add the bouillon cubes and three-fourths of the amount of water recommended in the brown rice package directions (or 1¾ cups).
4. Pour into a lightly-oiled baking pan, cover with foil and bake in preheated oven 1 hour or until the rice has absorbed the liquid.
5. Prepare the wild rice mix according to package directions but using only three-fourths of the water specified. Pour into a lightly-oiled baking dish, cover and bake in preheated oven 1 hour.
6. Combine both rices in a large bowl, blending together with the poultry seasoning. The rice should look dry, not wet.

Sauce

6 cups ***CHICKEN STOCK***
3 chicken bouillon cubes
Roux *(see page 44)*
½ cup cream
¼ cup dry sherry

Put the *CHICKEN STOCK* and bouillon cubes in a large saucepan and heat. Add the *ROUX* and whisk to thicken. Add the cream and sherry and heat through.

CHICKEN STOCK

2 pounds chicken backs, wings, necks and bones
2 quarts cold water
1 onion, halved
2 carrots, cut in thirds
3 stalks celery with leaves, halved
1 bay leaf
6 crushed black peppercorns
1 teaspoon dried thyme
Salt

1. Wash the chicken parts under cold running water and place in a large stockpot or kettle. Add the water and remaining ingredients except salt.
2. Bring to a boil over high heat, removing the scum from the surface as it accumulates. Reduce the heat and simmer the stock, partially covered, 1 to 1½ hours.
3. Strain and allow the stock to cool to room temperature, uncovered. Taste and season with salt. Refrigerate overnight.
4. When ready to use, remove any solidified fat from the surface of the stock.

Note: This recipe makes about 7 cups. Unused stock may be frozen.

STIR-FRIED FRESH VEGETABLE MEDLEY IN GARLIC BUTTER

2 cups cauliflower florets
2 cups broccoli florets
2 to 3 medium-size carrots, peeled
½ cup clarified butter
1 to 2 cloves garlic, crushed
1 cup sliced zucchini

1. Slice the cauliflower and broccoli florets carefully to retain the cross-section of the "flower" in each slice. Slice the carrots into 3" juliennes.
2. Heat the clarified butter in a wok or skillet. Add the garlic and sauté gently over medium heat.
3. Add the carrots and cauliflower and sauté 5 minutes.
4. Add the broccoli and zucchini and sauté 5 minutes, or until all vegetables are cooked to desired tenderness (slightly under-done is preferred). Serve immediately.

Note: The vegetables may be prepared for cooking well in advance, but the cooking itself must be done at the last minute.

The trick to this recipe is to balance the cooking time so that the carrots and cauliflower become crisp-tender without overcooking the broccoli and zucchini. The vegetables should not become mushy.

The wine list at the Boulevard Inn is a California wine lover's dream. "I feature mostly California wines because I'm tired of high-priced French wine lists that few people can understand. I want the diner to know which wine he is ordering. I want to offer him a good wine with his dinner, one in the $8 to $10 range, encouraging him to experiment."

PASHKA WITH RASPBERRY MELBA SAUCE

1 pound cream cheese, softened
¼ cup sour cream
1 cup powdered sugar
½ teaspoon vanilla
1 egg yolk
½ cup dried currants
Raspberry Melba Sauce

1. Place the cream cheese, sour cream, powdered sugar, vanilla and egg yolk in the work bowl of a food processor fitted with a steel blade. Process until creamy.
2. Put the cheese mixture in a bowl and stir in the currants. Divide the mixture among 6 saucer-shaped champagne glasses, filling almost to the top of each glass. Chill
3. Top each dessert with **Raspberry Melba Sauce** and serve immediately.

This is a special recipe of Russian influence. I found it in a Napa Valley restaurant and spent some time developing it to perfection. There is no graininess when powdered sugar is used.

Raspberry Melba Sauce

1 (10-ounce) package frozen raspberries
1 to 2 tablespoons cornstarch

1. Drain the raspberry juice into a jar with a lid. (Save the raspberries for another use, such as over ice cream). Stir the cornstarch gradually into the juice. Put the lid on the jar and shake to combine.
2. Pour the contents of the jar into a saucepan and heat until the sauce thickens. Cool at room temperature before using.

Strothmann believes that the most important part of home cooking and entertaining is planning. "Take your guests' likes and dislikes into mind," he urges. "Too many people don't think about the menu well enough in advance. Sometimes they aren't realistic about the courses they select. If they choose dishes that will keep them running from the dining room to the kitchen, their guests won't be very comfortable," he says.

He prefers to have appetizers ready when guests arrive, served with wine in the living room, allowing relaxation and conversation. "I can slip out to the kitchen for a few last-minute preparations while they are talking," Strothmann says. He also urges home cooks not to plan too much food. "If I'm serving a soup, I might not serve a salad. Or if a heavy entrée is on the menu, I'll many times plan just a salad and a light dessert to complete the meal."

Del Mondo Ristorante

Dinner for Four

Mozzarella Marinara

Zuppa di Cozze

Mushroom Salad

Veal Scaloppine Marsala

Zucchini Grande

Chilled Zabaglione Cream

Campari

Wine:
Ruffino Riserva Ducale Gold

Rick Falzarano and Leo Crivello, Proprietors
Tom Robinette and Antone Tomasello, Chefs

DEL MONDO RISTORANTE

Del Mondo Ristorante is a busy place where the food and service are excellent. Owners Rick Falzarano and Leo Crivello are determined that their patrons have a good time at their attractively decorated restaurant. The food is Italian and many of the dishes featured are ones Falzarano learned from his parents and his uncle, Rocco Petrini. Petrini was associated with the Brown Derby Restaurant, the Windsor Hotel and the Four Trees, all in Los Angeles, California.

It was Petrini who inspired Falzarano to pursue his interest in food and cooking. After twenty-five years in the restaurant business, Falzarano realized a dream in 1977 when he and Crivello opened Del Mondo Ristorante.

Falzarano manages the kitchen and dining room, working closely with Chefs Tom Robinette and Antone Tomasello, both trained by Falzarano. Crivello manages the bar and coordinates the wine service at the restaurant.

A good chef, in Falzarano's estimation, is one who takes the time to be particular about food preparation. "He must be sensitive and approach each dish as if he were making it for himself. A good chef puts his heart and soul into cooking."

1550 North Farwell Avenue

MOZZARELLA MARINARA

Oil for deep-frying
4 slices mozzarella cheese, each about 4½" by 3" by ⅜"
¼ cup flour (approximately)
2 eggs, lightly beaten
Seasoned Bread Crumbs
Marinara Sauce *(see next page)*
4 anchovy filets (optional)

1. Heat the oil in a deep-fryer to 375° to 400°.
2. Dip each cheese slice into the flour, then into the eggs. Repeat the process, then dip into **Seasoned Bread Crumbs.** Pat the crumbs into the cheese, making sure all sides are well coated.
3. Deep-fry the cheese slices about 2 minutes or until golden brown. Drain. Place each slice on a serving plate and spoon **Marinara Sauce** over cheese. Lay an anchovy filet across each, if desired.

Seasoned Bread Crumbs

1 cup dry bread crumbs
¼ cup freshly grated imported Romano cheese
⅛ teaspoon salt
Pinch of freshly ground black pepper
1½ teaspoons dried parsley flakes
Pinch of garlic powder

Combine all ingredients.

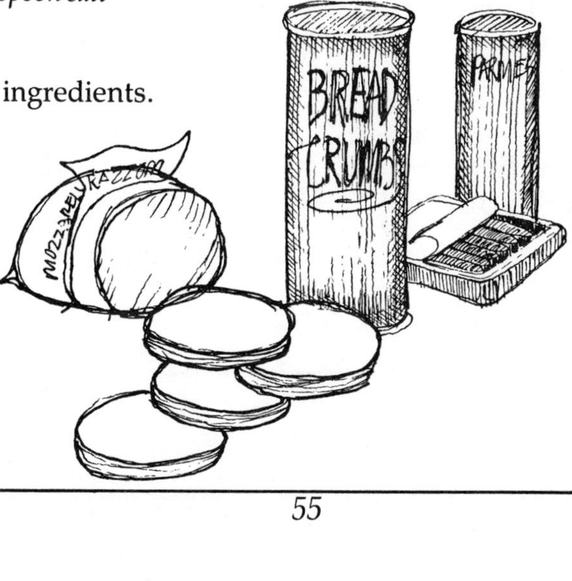

Marinara Sauce

2 teaspoons vegetable oil
1 clove garlic
½ large onion, diced
3 to 4 small cubes pork (optional)
2 cups canned or fresh chopped tomato, including juice
1 cup water
1 bay leaf
¼ teaspoon sweet basil
¼ teaspoon salt
Pinch of freshly ground black pepper

1. Heat the oil in a skillet over medium heat. Add the garlic, onion and (optional) pork cubes. Sauté 5 minutes or until the onions are translucent, but not brown. Remove the garlic clove.
2. Increase heat to medium and add the tomato, water, bay leaf, basil, salt and pepper. When the mixture starts to bubble, reduce heat to low and simmer, uncovered for 30 minutes.

Note: The Seasoned Bread Crumbs can be prepared in advance, as can the Marinara Sauce. Also, the cheese can be prepared, covered and refrigerated through step 2. If the sauce is prepared in advance, be sure to reheat it. Extra sauce is delicious on cooked pasta. Leftover Seasoned Bread Crumbs can be covered and refrigerated a few days and used in other cooking, or they can be frozen for future use.

Be sure to pack and cover the cheese slices well with the crumbs. It is important when you are deep-frying the cheese slices that the cheese not melt through the coating. After you have put the cheese in the hot oil, use tongs to keep it moving on the bottom of the pan. When it is done, it will rise to the surface of the oil.

ZUPPA DI COZZE

¼ cup coarsely chopped onion
1 teaspoon coarsely chopped celery
1 teaspoon coarsely chopped garlic
½ cup olive oil
1 tablespoon finely chopped fresh basil, or 1 teaspoon dry basil
Freshly ground black pepper
½ cup dry white wine
2 cups canned Italian plum or whole pack tomatoes, chopped, including juice
4 dozen small mussels in shells, scrubbed thoroughly
2 teaspoons freshly grated lemon peel

1. Combine the onions, celery and garlic on a cutting board and chop together very finely.
2. Heat the olive oil in a 3 to 4-quart saucepan. Add the chopped vegetables, basil and a few grindings of pepper. Cook over moderate heat, stirring frequently, 8 to 10 minutes.
3. Add the wine and boil briskly to reduce the mixture to about ¼ cup. Add the tomatoes and simmer uncovered about 20 minutes over low heat.
4. Add the mussels, cover the pan and cook over high heat 10 minutes. The mussels should open; if they do not, cook a few minutes longer. Discard any that remain closed. Serve immediately.

Note: The soup can be made ahead and warmed over medium heat. Do not make more than 1 day in advance.

Be sure to scrub the mussels well, so as to remove all of the beards.

MUSHROOM SALAD

¼ cup vegetable oil
1 teaspoon lemon juice
¼ teaspoon salt
Freshly ground black pepper
Pinch of garlic powder (optional)
¼ cup diced sweet onion (optional)
4 whole Italian olives (optional)
1 pound mushrooms, cleaned and chilled, sliced ⅛″

1. Blend the oil, lemon juice, salt, a pinch of black pepper, and, if desired, garlic powder, diced onion and olives in a small bowl.
2. Place the mushroom slices in a serving bowl. Pour the dressing over and mix gently.
3. Divide among 4 chilled salad plates and garnish each with a grinding of fresh black pepper.

Note: The salad can be made 1 to 2 hours ahead.

The secret to this recipe is selecting good-quality, white, firm mushrooms. Also, be sure to let them marinate in the dressing to pick up extra flavor.

VEAL SCALOPPINI MARSALA

8 (2-ounce) thin slices veal cutlet
½ cup flour
¼ pound butter
20 mushrooms, sliced
⅔ cup sweet Marsala wine
Chopped parsley for garnish

1. Pound the veal with a mallet to break down the veins and make it even and thin. Dip each slice in the flour. Pat between hands to remove excess flour.
2. Melt the butter over medium heat in a skillet, taking care not to burn it. When the butter sizzles, sauté the veal slices 1 to 2 minutes until juices show on top of the meat.
3. Using a spatula and spoon, turn the veal slices. Add the mushrooms. Sauté the veal 1 or 2 minutes more, until lightly browned on the edges. Do not overcook.
4. Add the wine. Tilt the pan and hold the veal and mushrooms on the high side with the spatula so veal is away from heat and wine mixture is near heat. Shake the pan to flame the wine (use a match if stove is electric).
5. Simmer about 3 minutes or until syrupy, occasionally dipping the pan to flavor the veal with sauce.
6. Place the veal on a heated serving platter. Pour the sauce over and sprinkle with parsley. Serve immediately.

Note: The veal can be prepared in advance through step 1. Cooking must be done at the last minute.

It is important to pound the veal so it is of uniform thickness, and therefore will cook evenly.

ZUCCHINI GRANDE

1 (5 to 8-pound) zucchini
¼ cup olive oil
Salt
1 large onion, finely chopped
1 pound lean ground beef
½ cup canned tomato sauce
½ teaspoon thyme
¾ teaspoon salt
3 cups diced french bread
1 (12-ounce) package Swiss chard, finely chopped
¼ cup freshly grated Parmesan cheese, plus more to taste
3 eggs
¼ cup lightly packed parsley

1. Slice the zucchini in half lengthwise; reserve one half for another use. Scoop the soft, seedy center from the remaining half; discard. Score the flesh in 1" squares, cutting halfway through to the outer skin. Rub with 2 tablespoons olive oil and sprinkle lightly with salt. Set aside.
2. To make the filling, heat 2 tablespoons olive oil in a wide skillet. Add the onion and cook until soft, stirring. Add the meat, breaking it apart with a spoon, and cook over high heat until browned. Add the tomato sauce, thyme and salt and simmer 5 minutes, stirring occasionally. Remove from heat and set aside.
3. Preheat oven to 325°.
4. Cover the bread with water; drain. Using your hands, squeeze out as much water as possible. Set aside.
5. Combine the meat sauce, bread, chard, ¼ cup Parmesan cheese, eggs and parsley. Beat to blend. Mound the mixture into the zucchini half, patting firmly in place.
6. Place the zucchini in a baking pan and add ½" water. Bake uncovered 1¼ hours in preheated oven.
7. Transfer the zucchini to a cutting board. Cut crosswise into serving portions. Serve with extra Parmesan cheese as topping.

Note: The zucchini can be made ahead, covered and reheated in a 325° oven 15 to 20 minutes. The remaining half of the zucchini can be used raw in salads, as part of a crudite (raw vegetable) tray or in other recipes.

CHILLED ZABAGLIONE CREAM

6 tablespoons sugar
1 teaspoon unflavored gelatin
½ cup Marsala wine
3 eggs, separated
3 egg yolks
1 tablespoon brandy
1 tablespoon vanilla
1 cup whipping cream
¼ teaspoon salt
¼ teaspoon cream of tartar
½ ounce semisweet chocolate, shaved into curls

1. Mix 4 tablespoons sugar and the gelatin in a measuring cup. Stir in the wine. Set aside.
2. Place all 6 egg yolks in the top of a double broiler and beat until thick and light in color. Stir in the gelatin mixture.
3. Place over hot water and cook, stirring constantly, until thickened. Remove from heat. Stir in the brandy and vanilla. Chill until cool, but not set. Stir occasionally.
4. Whip the cream until stiff. Fold into the egg yolk mixture.
5. Beat the egg whites until foamy. Add the salt and cream of tartar. Beat until stiff. Beat in 2 tablespoons sugar.
6. Fold the whites into the cream/egg yolk mixture. Spoon into 6 to 8 tall parfait glasses or dessert dishes. Chill 1 hour or longer.
7. Garnish with chocolate curls.

Note: The remaining 2 servings can be covered, refrigerated, and served within a day or two.

Be sure not to overfold the whipped cream and the stiffly-beaten egg whites. Have patience with step 3. The mixture will thicken.

CAMPARI

½ cup Campari
20 ounces seltzer water
Ice cubes

Mix 1 ounce Campari to 5 ounces seltzer for each drink. Serve over ice in tall glasses as after-dinner drinks.

The English Room

Dinner for Four

Fonds d'Artichauts en Couronne

Bouillabaisse Marseillaise

Salad of Mushrooms and Chicken Livers

Mignons et Ris de Veau aux Chanterelles

Braised Lettuce

Crêpes Flambées Foret Noire

Wine:

With the Artichokes—Meursalt-Charmes, 1976
With the Veal—Moulin-a-Vent, Lanvin, 1978

The Marcus Corporation, Proprietor
Uwe Henze, Maître de Cuisine

ENGLISH ROOM

The English Room is well known in Milwaukee for fine dining. Located in the Pfister Hotel, the English Room has changed with the times to reflect trends in food and service. In the early '70s, it switched its emphasis from a steak-house operation to a fine dining room with two different menus. Then, in 1977, the English Room was renovated to include dark paneling, traditional tapestry fabrics and plush burgundy carpeting. The valuable collection of late nineteenth century art was moved from the old English Room into its present-day counterpart. The atmosphere is cozy, warm, intimate and friendly.

The menu also was changed, taking on vast listings of cold and hot appetizers, fish and seafood entrées, meat entrées, game and poultry items, salads, vegetables and potato dishes and desserts. Through the menu changes, the English Room never abandoned its dedication to superb food cooked to order and fine service.

The menu is heavily French with all items served tableside. Some items are cooked tableside, as well. Maître d'Hôtel Frank Bonfiglio is well identified with the English Room and he shows his flair during tableside cooking. Keeping up with the times, the English Room also offers touches of nouvelle cuisine. The concept involves combining the freshest foods with low-fat ingredients in a new classic manner.

Maître de Cuisine Uwe Henze is responsible for food preparation in the English Room as well as throughout the hotel. He began his food training in Bremen, Germany, when he was fifteen. He received his degree in hotel-motel management at the Culinary School in Bremen, and served a four-year apprenticeship at the famed Park Hotel in that city. He also cooked in restaurants and hotels in Massachusetts, New York, Pennsylvania and Louisiana before joining the Marcus Hotel Corporation in 1976. He has won many awards for his cooking.

424 East Wisconsin Avenue

FONDS D'ARTICHAUTS EN COURONNE

10 ounces king crab meat
1½ teaspoons chopped shallots
1 cup sliced mushrooms
¼ teaspoon paprika
¾ cup dry white wine
½ teaspoon dry mustard
1 cup milk
Salt
Freshly ground white pepper
Pinch of thyme
1 tablespoon butter, room temperature
1 tablespoon flour
¼ cup cream
8 cooked artichoke bottoms
Sauce Maison *(see next page)*

1. Thaw the crab meat, if frozen. Press dry.
2. Sauté the shallots and mushrooms in butter in a 1-quart saucepan. Do not brown.
3. Add the paprika and wine. Bring to a boil and simmer to reduce by one-half.
4. Soak the mustard in the milk 2 minutes. Add to the sauce. Season with salt and pepper to taste and thyme.
5. Return to a boil. Combine the butter and flour to form a paste and add to the sauce, stirring constantly to combine. Add the crab meat and cream. Stir to combine.
6. Place 2 artichoke bottoms on each of 4 plates. Mound the crab meat filling atop the artichoke bottoms. Divide the **Sauce Maison** over the stuffed artichoke bottoms. Put the plates under a hot broiler for a few minutes to brown the sauce.

Note: This recipe can be made in advance to the point of running the assembled servings under the broiler to brown the sauce.

Sauce Maison

1 cup BÉARNAISE SAUCE
¼ cup tomato paste
¼ cup grated Parmesan cheese

Combine all ingredients.

BÉARNAISE SAUCE

1 cup dry white wine
1 tablespoon tarragon vinegar
1 tablespoon finely chopped shallots
2 small stalks tarragon, coarsely chopped, or 1 teaspoon dried tarragon
1 small sprig parsley
1 teaspoon dried chervil
2 black peppercorns, crushed
3 egg yolks, lightly beaten
1 cup butter, melted
Dash of cayenne pepper

1. Combine the wine, vinegar, shallots, tarragon, parsley, chervil and peppercorns in a saucepan. Cook over high heat until reduced by one-third. Strain and cool slightly.
2. Beating constantly and vigorously with a whisk, add the yolks alternately with the butter until the sauce is the consistency of heavy cream.
3. Add the cayenne pepper and stir to mix.

BOUILLABAISSE MARSEILLAISE

½ cup olive oil
2 cups chopped onion
8 cloves garlic, chopped
½ cup celery, julienned
½ cup carrot, julienned
2 cups leek (white only), julienned
½ cup chopped parsley
⅛ bay leaf
2 cups chopped tomatoes
Rind of ¾ orange
2 tablespoons fennel or anise seeds
Pinch of cayenne pepper
Pinch of ground black pepper
Pinch of salt
½ pound red snapper, boned
¼ pound codfish, boned
¼ pound scallops
½ pound shrimp
4 pieces lobster tail
2 quarts **Fish Stock** *(see next page)*
¼ teaspoon saffron
3 cups dry white wine
Pinch of thyme

1. Put the oil in a large soup kettle and sauté the onion, garlic, celery, carrot and leek 2 to 3 minutes.
2. Add the remaining ingredients except the saffron, wine and thyme. Cover and bring to a boil. Lower the heat and simmer 15 minutes.
3. Add the saffron, wine and thyme and simmer 5 minutes more. Taste and adjust seasoning if necessary. Remove the orange rind and serve at once, taking care to distribute the seafood evenly.

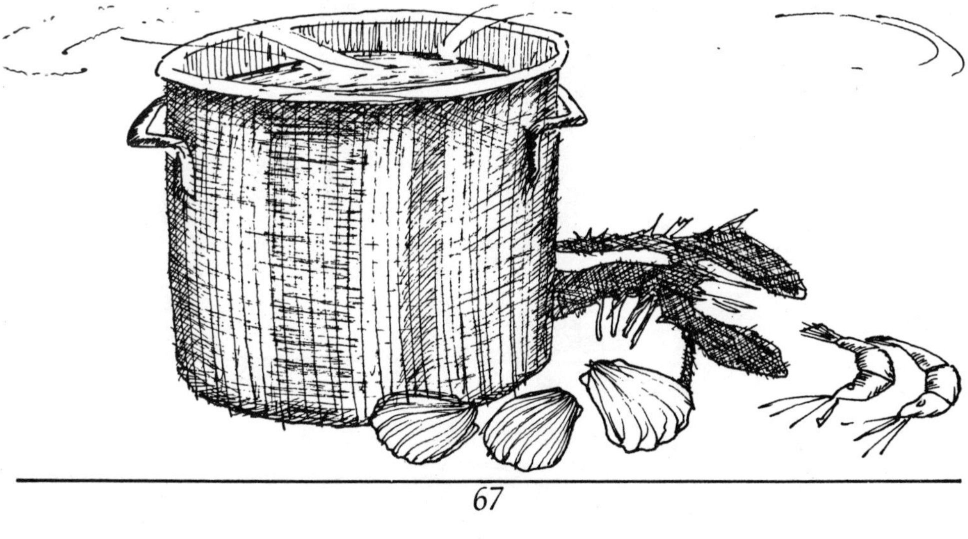

Fish Stock

2 pounds raw fish bones and trimmings, chopped
1 onion, minced
Few sprigs parsley
10 black peppercorns
1 quart dry white wine
1 quart water
Pinch of salt

Place all ingredients in a large stockpot. Cover and simmer gently 25 minutes on medium-high heat. Strain before using.

Note: The Fish Stock can be made in advance and frozen. The Bouillabaisse can be made in advance through step 1. Complete the recipe shortly before serving. Leftover Bouillabaisse will keep for 1 to 2 days if it is tightly covered and refrigerated. To reheat, simmer gently until heated through.

SALAD OF MUSHROOMS AND CHICKEN LIVERS

3 ounces chicken livers, cleaned, cut in small pieces
Salt and feshly ground black pepper
Pinch of thyme
¼ cup olive oil
2 cups mushrooms, cleaned
1 bunch watercress, cleaned and crisped
Vinaigrette Sauce
1 head Boston lettuce, cleaned and crisped
8 green asparagus, cooked crisp-tender

1. Sprinkle the livers with salt, pepper and thyme.
2. Put the olive oil in a sauté pan and cook the livers over medium-high heat, stirring constantly until done, 3 to 5 minutes. Remove from the pan and set aside.
3. Sauté the mushrooms in the same sauté pan 5 to 10 minutes. Remove and set aside.
4. Combine the chicken livers, mushrooms, watercress and **Vinaigrette Sauce**. Set aside.
5. Divide the lettuce among 4 salad plates. Place 2 spears of asparagus on each plate and divide the chicken liver mixture evenly among the plates. Serve immediately.

Vinaigrette Sauce

¼ cup chopped shallots
½ cup red wine vinegar
½ cup walnut oil
2 tablespoons chopped chives

Mix all ingredients together well.

MIGNONS ET RIS DE VEAU
aux Chanterelles

¾ pound blanched sweetbreads, membranes removed
4 (3-ounce) slices veal scaloppini, pounded thin
¼ cup walnut oil
2 tablespoons chopped shallots
¼ cup dry white wine
3 tablespoons Madeira
¼ cup cream
½ cup Veal Stock (see index)
¼ pound chanterelles
¼ cup low-fat ricotta cheese
1 teaspoon low-fat plain yogurt

1. Sauté the sweetbreads and veal in the walnut oil over high heat, 1 minute on each side. Remove from the pan and set aside in a warm oven.
2. Add the shallots to the pan and sauté until translucent. Do not brown.
3. Add the white wine and Madeira and cook over high heat 1 minute to reduce in volume. Add the cream and Veal Stock and cook over medium heat until slightly reduced, or until the sauce is of medium thickness.
4. Add the chanterelles. Mix the ricotta and yogurt together and blend into the sauce.
5. Place the veal and sweetbreads on a warm platter and pour the sauce over. Serve immediately.

Note: To blanch the sweetbreads, soak in cold water 1 hour. Drain, place in saucepan and cover with fresh water. Bring to a boil, reduce heat and simmer 10 to 15 minutes. Drain well. Run under cold water. Drain and remove the connective and covering tissues. Place on a plate and put another plate on top, weighted down so as to flatten the sweetbreads. Refrigerate to cool.

BRAISED LETTUCE

1 head romaine lettuce, cleaned, leaves separated
1 medium-size carrot, peeled and julienned
2 ribs celery, julienned
1 medium-size onion, julienned
1 cup Veal Stock (see index)

1. Preheat oven to 325°.
2. Put the romaine leaves in boiling salted water to blanch, 2 to 3 minutes. Drain into a colander and run the colander under cold running water to stop the cooking of the lettuce leaves.
3. Cook the carrots, celery and onion in the Veal Stock 3 minutes. Strain, saving both juice and vegetables.
4. Divide the vegetable mixture over the centers of the romaine leaves. Fold the sides of each leaf over and roll to contain the vegetables.
5. Place the rolled leaves in a pan and cover with the reserved Veal Stock in which the vegetables were cooked. Cover with foil.
6. Place in preheated oven and braise 10 minutes. Remove and serve.

CREPES FLAMBEES FORET NOIRE

8 cooked **Dessert Crêpes**
1½ pints vanilla ice cream, softened (approximately)
1¼ cups sugar
1½ cups dry red wine
4 whole cloves
2 cinnamon sticks
2 teaspoons orange zest
½ pound frozen raspberries, thawed
½ cup Kirsch
¼ cup sliced almonds

1. Fill each crêpe with softened ice cream, rolling to enclose the ice cream. Freeze, well covered, until ready to use.
2. Heat a sauté pan and add the sugar, cooking until light caramel in color. Add the wine, cloves, cinnamon and orange zest. Cook until reduced and slightly thickened. Remove the cloves, cinnamon and zest.
3. Add the raspberries and cook until smooth and a glaze results. Add the Kirsch and flame.
4. Place 2 filled crêpes on each of 4 plates and dress with sauce. Garnish with the almonds. Serve immediately.

Dessert Crêpes

1⅛ cups sifted flour
1 tablespoon sugar
Pinch of salt
3 eggs, beaten
1½ cups milk
1 tablespoon melted butter
1 tablespoon Cognac

1. Sift the flour, sugar and salt together into a bowl.
2. Combine the eggs and milk and stir into the dry ingredients until the batter is smooth. Stir in the butter and Cognac.
3. Let the batter stand 2 hours.
4. Heat a 5 to 6-inch skillet or crêpe pan and coat with butter. Remove the pan from the heat and pour in 1½ tablespoons batter. Tilt and rotate the pan to cover the bottom with batter. Return the pan to the heat 1 to 2 minutes or until the bottom of the crêpe is browned. Do not overcook.
5. Slide onto a rack to cool. Repeat until batter is gone. Extra crêpes may be used in other recipes.

Note: The crêpes should be made in advance. Cooked crêpes can be stored in the refrigerator, stacked on top of each other, separated by wax paper. They also can be frozen if tightly wrapped. Crêpes filled with ice cream can be assembled and frozen up to 1 week in advance if very tightly wrapped.

The Fox and Hounds

Dinner for Six

Vegetable Aspic

Clear Beef Consommé

Salad with Hot Bacon Dressing

Roast Goose Breasts

Baked Cauliflower

Chocolate Mousse

Wine:

With the Aspic—Simi Chardonnay, 1974
With the Goose—Gevrey-Chambertin, Les Petit Chapelles, 1969
With the Mousse—Piesporter Guenthersaly Marienhof
"Eiswein," Beerenauslese,
Q/P Bildesheim, 1973

Karl Ratzsch Jr., Proprietor
Josef Ratzsch, General Manager
Lee Lederhause, Chef

FOX AND HOUNDS

The Fox and Hounds in Hubertus, about 25 miles northwest of downtown Milwaukee, offers a total experience in dining. Nestled in Kettle Moraine country, the Fox and Hounds gives the impression of an eighteenth century English lodge. The original dining room was once a one-room log cabin, built in 1845. Stylish additions develop the lodge feeling in this restaurant decorated with plants, antique glassware and china, a giant wrought-iron chandelier and an enormous stone fireplace.

The restaurant is owned by Karl Ratzsch, Jr., who is also affiliated with Ratzsch's in downtown Milwaukee, where German food is served. The cuisine at the Fox and Hounds is more early American but with some German touches, especially evident in the goose and sausage dishes. Country-oven dinners are featured at the Fox and Hounds and the servings are indeed ample.

Chef Lee Lederhause has an associate degree in cooking from Milwaukee Area Technical College. Lederhause has been cooking since he was sixteen, and he apprenticed in 1965 under two chefs at Milwaukee's now-defunct Plankinton Hotel. Since 1967, he has worked at the Fox and Hounds. The ability to be creative is most important if a chef is to be good, Lederhause believes. He lends that to the Fox and Hounds, and his particular area of interest within cooking is in making sauces.

1298 Friess Lake Road
Hubertus

VEGETABLE ASPIC

½ cup chopped carrot
½ cup chopped onion
½ cup dry white wine
4 sprigs parsley
¼ cup celery leaves
¼ bay leaf
¼ teaspoon salt
½ medium-size tomato
2 envelopes unflavored gelatin
¼ cup cold water
6 thin horizontal slices peeled cucumber
3 medium-size carrots, pared, julienned 1"
⅓ cup shredded red cabbage
1 medium-size zucchini, finely chopped
Lettuce leaves, cleaned

1. Place the carrot, onion, wine, parsley sprigs, celery leaves, bay leaf, salt and tomato in a large stockpot or saucepan. Add 1 quart water and simmer gently 20 to 30 minutes.
2. Strain and discard all the vegetables and spices. Cool the broth slightly and strain again through fine cheesecloth. Set aside.
3. Dissolve the gelatin in the cold water. Slowly add to the vegetable stock, stirring over low heat until the gelatin is completely dissolved.
4. Pour ¼" aspic into the bottom of 6 custard cups. Chill until firm. Reserve the remaining aspic at room temperature.
5. Poach the cucumber, carrots, cabbage and zucchini separately in boiling salted water until just crisp-tender, 2 to 3 minutes each. Drain very thoroughly and set each aside.
6. Remove the custard cups from refrigerator. Dip each cucumber slice in the room-temperature aspic and place on the firm aspic in the bottoms of the cups. Gently pour ¼" aspic over the cucumber in each cup. Refrigerate until firm.
7. Remove the custard cups from refrigerator. Dip the juliennes of carrot in the room-temperature aspic and stand the carrot sticks up around the rims of the custard cups, dividing the carrots evenly among the cups. Divide the red cabbage among the cups, placing it over the aspic, within the carrot sticks. Fill the cups with aspic to the tops of the carrot sticks and refrigerate until firm.

(continued next page)

8. Remove the custard cups from refrigerator. Divide the chopped zucchini among the cups and top with the remaining aspic. Refrigerate until set.
9. To serve, dip the cups into warm water and unmold each onto lettuce-lined plates. Serve immediately.

Prepared vegetable aspic will last several weeks in the refrigerator if tightly covered in the custard cups. Be sure not to overcook the vegetables that are molded into the aspic.

CLEAR BEEF CONSOMME

1 quart water
1½ pounds beef bones, washed in cold water
2 medium-size carrots, peeled
1 large onion, halved
1 clove garlic
1 stalk celery

Bouquet Garni
1 bay leaf
3 sprigs parsley
Pinch of thyme
Dash of salt
Pinch of ground black pepper
1 cup dry red wine
Croutons

1. Place the water, bones, carrots, onion, garlic, celery, **Bouquet Garni,** bay leaf, parsley and thyme in a large stockpot. Bring to a simmer very slowly and allow to simmer 3 to 3½ hours, uncovered.
2. Strain the consommé to remove the vegetables and seasonings. Allow to cool at room temperature. Refrigerate overnight.
3. Remove the solidified fat from the surface of the consommé. Put the consommé into a stockpot or large saucepan and add salt, pepper and wine. Bring to a simmer, but do not boil. Reduce the volume of the consommé slightly to intensify the flavor and to heat to serving temperature.
4. Divide among 6 soup bowls and garnish with croutons. Serve immediately.

Note: The consommé can be prepared in advance, frozen and reheated if desired. Be sure not to allow it to boil or it will become cloudy.

The quality of the consommé depends on good, flavorful bones.

Bouquet Garni

2 sprigs parsley
1 clove garlic
¼ teaspoon thyme
3 to 4 black peppercorns
Pinch of marjoram
½ bay leaf

Tie all ingredients in a cheesecloth bag.

SALAD WITH HOT BACON DRESSING

1 head iceberg lettuce, or 1 pound fresh spinach
12 slices bacon, coarsely chopped
1 medium-size onion, diced
3 cups warm Beef Stock (see index)
2 teaspoons sugar
½ cup red wine vinegar
Dash of brandy
2 tablespoons cornstarch
½ cup cold water
Salt and freshly ground black pepper to taste

1. If using iceberg lettuce, core, wash, dry and crisp the leaves. If using spinach, wash, stem and crisp the leaves.
2. Fry the bacon in a medium-size skillet until crisp. Add the onion and cook until tender, but not brown. Cool slightly.
3. Add the stock, sugar, vinegar and brandy and simmer over medium heat 20 minutes. Remove from heat and skim the fat from the surface.
4. Mix the cornstarch with the water. Return the dressing to heat and add the cornstarch mixture, stirring until thickened. Taste and correct the seasoning with salt and pepper if necessary.
5. Divide the lettuce or spinach leaves among 6 salad plates and pass the hot dressing at table.

Note: The dressing can be made in advance and gently reheated, if desired.

ROAST GOOSE BREASTS

2 (1½-pound) goose breasts
Salt and freshly ground black pepper
1 quart Chicken Stock (see index)
1 onion, sliced
1 carrot, peeled and chunked
1 teaspoon honey
1 cup dry white wine
Roux

1. Preheat oven to 450°.
2. Season the goose breasts with salt and pepper. Place in a baking pan and bake in preheated oven 35 minutes or until browned. Remove from oven and pour off the fat, reserving ¼ cup for **Roux.**
3. Add the Chicken Stock, onion, carrot, honey and wine to the pan. Return to the oven and cook 1 to 1½ hours or until the goose breasts are tender.
4. Remove the goose breasts to a serving platter and keep warm. Strain the pan drippings to remove the vegetables. Skim as much fat as possible from drippings and place the drippings in a saucepan. Gradually add the **Roux**, stirring constantly, until very thick.
5. Slice the goose breasts thinly. Pour the sauce over and serve immediately.

Roux

¼ cup reserved goose fat
¾ cup flour

Place the fat in a skillet and heat until sizzling. Add the flour and cook 2 to 3 minutes, stirring constantly with a wooden spoon. Remove from heat.

The important part of this recipe is thoroughly cooking the fat out of the goose breasts so that they are not greasy.

BAKED CAULIFLOWER

1 large head cauliflower, washed and trimmed into small florets
1 tablespoon butter
1 tablespoon flour
Salt
Freshly ground white pepper
¼ cup grated Parmesan cheese
Dash of paprika
¼ cup toasted bread crumbs
⅛ cup slivered almonds, toasted

1. Preheat oven to 375.°
2. Place the florets in a large pan and just barely cover with water. Bring to a boil, reduce heat and cook until two-thirds done. Strain, saving both the liquid and the cauliflower. Place the cauliflower in a small casserole dish.
3. Heat the butter in a saucepan. When bubbling, add the flour and cook, stirring constantly, 2 to 3 minutes. Slowly add the cauliflower liquid and stir until slightly thickened. Season with salt, white pepper, Parmesan and paprika. Pour over the cauliflower in the casserole.
4. Bake in preheated oven 10 to 15 minutes. Sprinkle with the bread crumbs and almonds and serve immediately.

Note: This dish can be prepared in advance through step 2. Bring it to room temperature if refrigerated and bake in preheated 400° oven 10 to 15 minutes.

Take care not to overcook the cauliflower in the first step of this recipe.

CHOCOLATE MOUSSE

1½ teaspoons unflavored gelatin
2 tablespoons cold water
1 cup milk
2 (1-ounce) squares unsweetened chocolate, shaved
¾ cup sugar
½ teaspoon salt
1 teaspoon vanilla extract
2 cups whipping cream, whipped

1. Mix the gelatin and water, stirring until the gelatin is completely dissolved.
2. Place the milk in a saucepan and scald. Add the chocolate shavings and stir to dissolve. Blend in the gelatin mixture. Remove from heat.
3. Add the sugar and salt and mix until well blended. Allow the mixture to cool. Stir in the vanilla.
4. Fold the whipped cream into the chocolate mixture and pour into a 9″ x 12″ pan. Freeze until firm. To serve, scoop into large balls using a spoon and place in tall wine glasses, or cut into squares and serve.

Note: Any leftover dessert can be covered well with plastic wrap and returned to the freezer to serve within the next few days.

Whipping Cream
Sugar

Grenadier's Restaurant

Dinner for Six

Escargots Bon Maman

Bavarian Lentil Soup

Artichoke Salad

Calcutta Lamb Curry with Chutney and Kumquats

Cold Vegetable Pâté

Israeli Date Dessert

Wine:

With the Escargot–Morgon Grand Cru Beaujolais
Ets R. Doucet, 1978
With the Lamb–Muscadet, Chatelain-Desjaques, 1978

Bob and Dave Jordan and Knut Apitz, Proprietors
Knut Apitz, Executive Chef

GRENADIER'S RESTAURANT

Grenadier's is a well-appointed restaurant with an inviting decor and innovative cooking as its trademark. Owned by Bob and Dave Jordon of Jordan Engineering & Tool Sales Co., and Executive Chef Knut Apitz, the six-year-old downtown restaurant tries to please every diner on his level. "We respond to the individual customer's needs, using the freshest and best of ingredients," says Apitz. He and his staff make practically everything that is served in the restaurant on the premises.

All of the dishes served at Grenadier's are the inspiration or development of Apitz. Born in Berlin, he served as a chef's apprentice for three years, followed by another three years of schooling before his graduation in 1957. He has worked in restaurant kitchens in the Black Forest, Switzerland, Holland, England and the United States.

"A good chef loves people and enjoys cooking," says Apitz, and adds, "I am constantly learning." He believes that the hardest part of making a meal at home is being restricted by limited kitchen space and lack of ingredients, such as stocks and sauces which are on hand at all times in good restaurants.

747 North Broadway

ESCARGOTS BON MAMAN

36 large mushrooms, stems removed
4 tablespoons butter
Pinch of salt
½ teaspoon finely chopped shallots
36 escargots
½ cup dry red wine
1½ cups **Brown Sauce**
½ teaspoon chopped garlic
1 teaspoon chopped parsley

1. Sauté the mushroom caps in butter in a sauté pan over medium heat. Add the salt. Remove the caps from the pan with a slotted spoon and divide among 6 escargot dishes. Keep warm.
2. Sauté the shallots in the same pan for 20 seconds; add the escargots. Increase heat, add the wine and cook 30 seconds. Add the **Brown Sauce.**
3. Remove the escargots with a slotted spoon and place in the mushroom caps. Keep warm.
4. Reduce the sauce over high heat 1 minute. Reduce heat to medium and add the garlic and parsley. Mix together. Lightly spoon the sauce over the mushrooms and escargots and serve immediately.

Brown Sauce

1½ tablespoons clarified butter
1½ tablespoons flour
2 cups Beef Stock (see index)

1. Melt the clarified butter in a saucepan and add the flour. Cook over low heat, stirring occasionally, until flour and butter are blended and about the color of brown wrapping paper.
2. Gradually stir in the Beef Stock. Bring the sauce to a boil and cook 3 to 5 minutes, stirring constantly. Lower heat and simmer sauce gently 30 minutes, stirring occasionally. Skim off fat and strain sauce through a fine sieve.

Note: This appetizer must be prepared just before it is to be served; however, all of the preliminary preparation can be completed so that the cooking will go quickly. Additional Brown Sauce can be frozen for use in other sauces.

When making the sauce for the escargots, watch it closely. It should be neither too thin nor too thick. The right consistency is when it just coats the back of a spoon.

BAVARIAN LENTIL SOUP

1½ cups lentils, thoroughly rinsed and picked over for stones, and soaked in 3 cups water overnight
1½ quarts Beef or Chicken Stock (see index)
¾ cup diced bacon
½ cup diced ham
½ medium-size onion, diced
1 medium-size carrot, peeled and diced
1 stalk celery, diced
1 teaspoon salt
½ teaspoon freshly ground black pepper
¾ cup red wine vinegar (approximately)
½ cup packed brown sugar
1 bay leaf

1. Drain the lentils and place them in a large kettle with the stock.
2. Fry the bacon in a large sauté pan until crisp. Add the diced ham, onion, carrot and celery. Sauté 2 minutes; add to kettle.
3. Season with the salt and pepper. Add the vinegar, brown sugar and bay leaf.
4. Cook the soup over medium heat until the lentils are tender, taking care not to break up the beans when stirring the soup.
5. Remove the bay leaf and serve immediately.

Note: The soup can be made in advance and reheated.

Be sure to wash the lentils thoroughly to remove sand and stones. You may want to add the vinegar and brown sugar to taste, possibly passing a cruet of vinegar and a bowl of brown sugar so that guests can adjust the taste of the soup to their own liking.

ARTICHOKE SALAD

12 canned artichoke hearts, cut in ½" pieces
1 cup sliced mushrooms
1 cup pea pods, tips and strings removed

Dressing
¾ cup toasted sliced almonds

1. Place the artichoke hearts, mushrooms and pea pods in a large salad bowl.
2. Carefully toss with enough **Dressing** to coat.
3. Gently stir in the toasted almonds just before serving on 6 salad plates.

Dressing

2 teaspoons Dijon mustard
1 teaspoon freshly ground black pepper
1 teaspoon salt
¼ cup red wine vinegar
¼ cup salad oil
1 teaspoon fresh or dried chopped dill
1 teaspoon finely chopped garlic
1 cup half-and-half or light cream

Mix the mustard, pepper, salt, vinegar, oil, dill and garlic in a small bowl. Slowly stir in the half-and-half. Taste and add more vinegar if desired.

Note: When cleaning the mushrooms, be sure to cut the bottom ⅛" off the stem. Very quickly wash in cold water to which you have added a little vinegar. This will help keep the mushrooms white. Dry thoroughly. To toast the almonds, put them in a baking pan in a preheated 350° oven for 10 to 15 minutes. Watch them carefully because they will burn easily. The salad can be assembled in advance and refrigerated, but it should not be dressed until serving time.

The pea pods, as well as the mushrooms, must be absolutely fresh. The mushrooms need only be medium-size, not large, but should be as white as possible.

CALCULTTA LAMB CURRY
with Chutney and Kumquats

1 (6-pound) leg or shoulder of lamb, boned (reserve bones), cubed 1"
Generous pinch of salt
1 bay leaf
Roux
¼ pound butter
2 medium-size onions, sliced
2 apples, peeled and julienned
¾ cup spicy Madras curry powder (approximately)
6 servings cooked rice or cooked noodles
12 kumquats
1 jar spicy chutney

1. Put the lamb bones in a large kettle and cover with water (about 2 quarts). Add the salt and bay leaf and cook 2 hours over medium heat, uncovered, removing scum from the surface of the stock as it rises.
2. Strain the stock into a saucepan and gradually stir in the **Roux** over medium heat until the stock thickens to the consistency of light cream soup. Set aside.
3. Preheat oven to 350°.
4. Melt the butter in a deep sauté pan. Add the onions and sauté over medium heat until glossy. Add the apples and sauté 3 minutes.
5. Lightly salt the lamb cubes and add to the onions and apples, sautéing and stirring 3 to 4 minutes over high heat.
6. Gradually add the curry powder, stirring and stopping to taste until the curry is to your liking. Cook 2 to 3 minutes.
7. Add the reserved sauce and bring to a boil. Cover and bake in preheated oven 30 to 45 minutes or until the lamb is fork-tender.
8. Serve over rice or noodles with kumquats and chutney.

Note: The entrée can be made in advance, reheated and then served over rice or noodles.

Be sure the lamb is at room temperature. For maximum flavor, the onions and apples must be sautéed before the meat is added to the pan. It's a good idea to add the curry powder gradually, stopping to taste, until the desired strength of curry is achieved. This will vary depending upon the kind of curry powder used.

Roux

4 tablespoons butter
4 tablespoons flour

Heat the butter in a sauté pan until it sizzles. Add the flour all at once. Stir with a spoon and cook 3 to 5 minutes.

COLD VEGETABLE PÂTÉ

¾ pound mushrooms, cleaned
1 tablespoon butter
Salt and freshly ground black pepper to taste
6 eggs
3 tablespoons unflavored gelatin
¾ pound carrots, peeled
½ teaspoon dill weed
1 pound spinach, washed and stemmed
Vegetable oil
Sauce Ravigote *(see next page)*

1. Cook the mushrooms in the butter in a sauté pan until all the moisture has evaporated. Add salt and pepper to taste. Pour the mushrooms into the work bowl of a food processor fitted with a steel blade. Add 2 eggs and 1 tablespoon unflavored gelatin. Process until smooth; set aside.
2. Poach the carrots in water to cover, adding the dill and salt and pepper to taste. When tender, drain and place carrots in the work bowl of the food processor fitted with the steel blade. Add 2 eggs and 1 tablespoon unflavored gelatin and process until smooth. Set aside.
3. Blanch the spinach in salted boiling water, then place under cold running water to stop cooking. Thoroughly drain, squeezing out all water. Place the spinach in the work bowl of food processor fitted with steel blade. Add 2 eggs and 1 tablespoon unflavored gelatin and process until smooth. Set aside.
4. Preheat oven to 400°.

(continued next page)

5. Lightly grease a 9" by 5" loaf pan with vegetable oil. Evenly smooth the mushroom mixture into the bottom of the pan. Top with the carrot mixture, smoothing evenly. Top with the spinach mixture, smoothing evenly.
6. Bake in preheated oven 1 hour or until a toothpick inserted in the center comes out clean.
7. The pâté can be served hot or allowed to cool. To serve, slice and place on individual plates. Pass **Sauce Ravigote** separately, allowing each person to add the desired amount of sauce.

Note: The pâté and sauce can be made in advance. The pâté will serve 10 to 12. It is impossible to reduce the quantity without affecting the quality of the recipe. Leftover pâté keeps well, covered and refrigerated, as does the sauce.

It is important when layering the vegetables for the pâté that each layer be as thick as the next. This does not affect the taste of the pâté, but will make it visually pleasing.

Sauce Ravigote

6 egg yolks
2 tablespoons mustard
1 teaspoon Worcestershire sauce
1 tablespoon lemon juice
3 leaves fresh spinach, washed, stemmed and finely chopped
3 cups salad oil

1. Place the egg yolks, mustard, Worcestershire sauce, lemon juice and spinach in the work bowl of a food processor fitted with a steel blade. Process 5 to 10 seconds.
2. With the machine running, slowly pour the oil through the feed tube until the sauce is thick.

ISRAELI DATE DESSERT

1½ cups honey
½ cup amaretto
24 dates, pitted and quartered
6 scoops butter pecan ice cream
¾ cup toasted sliced almonds

1. Stir the honey and amaretto together in a bowl. Add the dates and marinate at room temperature 1 hour.
2. Place 1 scoop ice cream in each of 6 bowls. Divide the date sauce evenly among the bowls. Sprinkle with toasted almonds and serve immediately.

Jack Pandl's
WHITEFISH BAY
Inn

Dinner for Six

Pandl's Vegetable Quiche

Chicken Liver Dumpling Soup

Spinach Salad with Jack Pandl's Hot Bacon Dressing

Broiled Whitefish

Asparagus with Sautéed Cracker Crumbs

Jack Pandl's Famous German Pancake

Wine:

Piesporter Goldtröpfchen Spätlese

Jack Pandl, Proprietor
J. Christopher Jamrozy, Chef

JACK PANDL'S WHITEFISH BAY INN

Jack Pandl has followed the restaurant tradition his parents began in 1915 when they bought the Whitefish Bay Inn. The Inn is surrounded by homes today, but sixty-six years ago the area was occupied only by farms and by the old Pabst Whitefish Bay Resort—a fairground of beer gardens, picnic tables and a dance pavilion. Jack's mother Anna came from Austria to Milwaukee when she was sixteen, to work as a cook in a hotel. There she met John Pandl, nineteen and a waiter. They eventually married and worked in the hotel business until they bought the Inn, desiring to combine their efforts in the restaurant field.

The menu at Pandl's has changed since its early days, but the culinary influence of Anna Pandl remains. She continued to run the business after her husband's death in 1932 while raising her three daughters and two sons. She put in full days at the restaurant, making fine soups and desserts and supervising other food preparations.

Anna imparted her cooking skills to her family and co-workers until she died in 1967. Eventually, her youngest son Jack bought into the restaurant. Today, Jack's three children are also involved, preserving the family tradition. Jack and his wife Elaine have helped to preserve the history of the region at the Whitefish Bay Inn. One of the few Milwaukee-area restaurants to endure the test of time at its original location, it is virtually a landmark, reminiscent of an unhurried past. The building's appearance has remained basically unchanged since 1915. Inside, Tiffany lamps, oak tables, fresh flowers and antique beer steins enhance the cosy charm of the dining rooms.

"We are unique in that we are a family operation located in a residential area," Jack says. "The customer has to seek us out, and he does. We offer a homey atmosphere that is not contrived."

To home cooks, his advice is to keep the menu simple when entertaining and not to take on more courses than one can easily prepare. In a restaurant, Pandl believes that the timing of dishes requires special effort. "But," he adds, "the real proof of the pudding, as far as a restaurant or the home cook is concerned, is in the eating. The food must be superior."

1319 East Henry Clay Street
Whitefish Bay

PANDL'S VEGETABLE QUICHE

1 tablespoon butter
1 cube vegetable or chicken bouillon
1 green onion, chopped
1½ cups cauliflower, chopped ¾"
½ cup chopped tomato
½ teaspoon chopped parsley
½ cup shredded American cheese
½ cup shredded Swiss cheese
1 (8") partially-baked pie shell
¼ cup evaporated milk
3 eggs, beaten
½ teaspoon freshly ground black pepper
½ teaspoon Italian seasoning
½ tablespoon dry sherry

1. Preheat oven to 350°.
2. Melt the butter in a sauté pan and break up the bouillon cube in the butter.
3. Add the green onion and cauliflower and sauté until the cauliflower is crisp-tender. Add the tomato, parsley and both cheeses. Mix gently. Pour into the pie shell and smooth evenly.
4. Put the milk, eggs, pepper, Italian seasoning and sherry in a bowl and beat. Pour over the vegetable mixture in the pie shell and jiggle the pan to distribute the egg mixture evenly.
5. Bake in preheated oven 35 to 40 minutes. Cut into wedges and serve warm.

Note: It is important not to overcook the vegetables when sautéing them. This recipe can be made in advance, covered and refrigerated. To reheat, place in preheated 300° for 15 to 20 minutes until heated through.

CHICKEN LIVER DUMPLING SOUP

1½ quarts Chicken Stock (see index)
⅓ cup chopped celery
⅓ cup chopped onion
Dumpling Batter
⅓ cup chopped tomato
1 tablespoon chopped parsley

1. Put the Chicken Stock, celery and onion in a soup kettle. Bring to a boil.
2. Roll the dumpling batter into 1" balls and drop in the soup.
3. Add the tomatoes and parsley and cook until the dumplings are plump and float to the top of the soup, about 10 to 15 minutes. Stir occasionally so that the dumplings don't stick to the bottom of the pan.

Dumpling Batter

¼ pound chicken livers, ground
¾ pound ground beef
1 egg
1½ cups bread crumbs
1 tablespoon chopped parsley
1 teaspoon salt
1 teaspoon chicken soup base, or 1 chicken bouillon cube
½ teaspoon ground white pepper
½ teaspoon ground thyme

Mix all ingredients together until thoroughly combined. Refrigerate until ready to form dumplings.

Note: When rolling the dumplings, flour your hands lightly and the task will be easier and less messy. The dumplings can be formed in advance and the soup prepared through step 1. After the dumplings are added to the soup, stir them gently so they do not break.

FRESH SPINACH SALAD
with Jack Pandl's Hot Bacon Dressing

1¼ cups water
¾ cup sugar
¼ cup plus 2 tablespoons vinegar
⅛ teaspoon salt
½ teaspoon chicken soup base, or 1 chicken bouillon cube
¼ teaspoon ground white pepper
¼ pound smoked bacon, chopped
¼ cup chopped onion
¼ cup flour
¾ pound spinach, washed, stemmed and dried

1. Combine the water, sugar, vinegar, salt, soup base or bouillon cube and pepper in a saucepan. Heat to boiling and keep hot.
2. Brown the bacon in a skillet. Remove the bacon from the pan and set aside. Cook the onions in the bacon fat until soft; do not brown.
3. Add the flour to the skillet and cook 2 to 3 minutes, stirring constantly.
4. Add the onion mixture to the saucepan and stir until smooth. Simmer 5 minutes. Add the reserved bacon.
5. Divide the spinach leaves evenly among 6 bowls. Pour the hot dressing over the spinach and serve at once.

Note: The dressing can be made ahead. To reheat, put it in the top of a double boiler over medium heat until hot. The dressing also can be poured over hot cooked potato slices to make German Potato Salad.

BROILED WHITEFISH

Vegetable oil
6 (8-ounce) whitefish filets, boned
Paprika
6 lemon wedges
Parsley

1. Line a baking sheet with foil and brush the foil with vegetable oil. Place the filets skin-side-down on the sheet and brush with oil.
2. Broil the filets 8 to 10 minutes or until the fish is flaky, but not dry. Sprinkle lightly with paprika.
3. Remove from the sheet with a spatula and place on plates. Garnish with lemon wedges and parsley.

Note: To debone whitefish filets, spread filets skin-side-down on a cutting board. Gently brush filets from head to tail with fingers to raise the bones. Use needle-nose pliers to pull the bones.

Take care not to overcook the fish.

ASPARAGUS WITH SAUTEED CRACKER CRUMBS

1½ pounds fresh asparagus
¼ pound butter
½ cup saltine crackers, coarsely crushed

1. Break tough ends off the asparagus and wash. Break into pieces, if desired, or leave whole.
2. Bring salted water to a boil and add the asparagus, cooking 10 to 12 minutes, or until the asparagus can be pierced easily with a sharp knife.
3. Melt the butter in a small saucepan and sauté the crumbs until browned.
4. Drain the asparagus and divide evenly among 6 plates. Top with the sautéed cracker crumbs.

Note: The crumbs can be sautéed in advance, but the asparagus must be cooked at the last moment.

Don't cover the asparagus while it is cooking or it will lose its bright green color. Don't overcook it, either.

JACK PANDL'S FAMOUS GERMAN PANCAKE

½ cup all-purpose flour
½ cup milk
Pinch of salt
4 large eggs
1 tablespoon butter
1 tablespoon shortening
Lemon wedges
Maple syrup
Powdered sugar
Butter

1. Mix the flour, milk and salt together in a mixing bowl until smooth. Add the eggs and beat until smooth.
2. Preheat oven to 425°.
3. Melt the butter and shortening in a 9" to 10" slope-sided pan with an ovenproof handle. Pour the batter into the pan and cook on the stove until the bottom of the pancake is browned, but uncooked batter remains on top, about 2 to 3 minutes.
4. With a spatula, turn the pancake quickly and make a criss-cross cut all the way through the pancake. Put in preheated oven about 12 minutes or until the edges are browned. The pancake will rise 3" to 5" all around the edges of the pan. The criss-cross cut will close as the pancake bakes.
5. Remove the pancake from the oven and quickly cut into 6 servings. Serve immediately with lemon, maple syrup, powdered sugar and butter.

Note: There should be some uncooked batter on top of the pancake before you turn it; however, the bottom should be cooked enough so that the pancake can be turned.

The pancake also can be served as an entrée with bacon or sausage.

JEAN PAUL
RESTAURANT FRANCAIS

Dinner for Six

Tortue du Wisconsin au Xérès

Crème de Moules au Safran

Salade Gourmande

Gambettes de Volaille au Sauternes

Gratin du Soleil

Coupe Meringuée aux Framboises

Wine:

With the Tortue–Sancerre, 1979
With the Volaille–young Barsac or Sauternes

Jean-Paul Weber, Proprietor and Chef

JEAN-PAUL RESTAURANT FRANCAIS

Creative cooking with an emphasis on nouvelle cuisine is the hallmark at Jean-Paul Restaurant Français. Chef and owner Jean-Paul Weber has been one of Milwaukee's leading restaurateurs since 1975, after having worked in a number of other prestigious establishments.

A native of Alsace, a border area where French and German cultures meld, Jean-Paul comes from a family long tied to restaurants. He has been employed at many European restaurants, most notably the famous Maxim's in Paris. He came to America in 1963, working in Chicago at Chez Paul among other places. He came to Milwaukee in 1972 as chef and manager of a then-new branch of Chez Paul.

"I think my restaurant is the only one of its kind in Milwaukee. And I would even go so far as to compare it to any of the top ten restaurants in this country," Jean-Paul states with pride. "Let me explain. In France, a one-star restaurant must have excellent food, a two-star must also have excellent service and a three-star requires both these qualities, plus excellent surroundings, like gardens, and so forth. I think I'm definitely in the two-star category."

"We make everything ourselves. No convenience food items are bought here," he says. Sauces are composed by reducing the liquids in which meat and fish are cooked. Intense in flavor, the sauces are then thickened with butter and, occasionally, puréed vegetables. Roux, used for thickening in classic French cooking, is not used at Jean-Paul.

Making good sauces is the most difficult part of home cooking, advises Jean-Paul. "The average home cook does not have the stocks, glazes and reductions on hand. He can make sauces without these, but they won't be as good. Equipment and space also can be a problem at home." In the restaurant, coordinating the help, planning and developing new dishes and keeping the whole venture in the profit realm frequently are big challenges," he adds. But the great pleasure of cooking is to be able to share it. "Without that, it's like catching the biggest fish or shooting a hole-in-one with no one around to share your experience," he says. "I love to watch for reaction to my cooking. It is my reward to watch a diner taste and enjoy, to see him smile and to catch the sparkle in the eye as he enjoys my creations."

811 East Wisconsin Avenue

TORTUE DU WISCONSIN
Au Xérès

4 to 6 slices white bread
Clarified butter
1½ pounds turtle meat or 2 cups boneless turtle meat
2 cups **Veal Stock** *(see next page) or Chicken Stock (see index)*
½ cup dry white wine
1 cup sliced mushrooms
¼ cup dry sherry
½ cup whipping cream
4 tablespoons unsalted butter
Salt and freshly ground white pepper
Chopped fresh parsley for garnish

1. With a 3" cookie cutter (or drinking glass), cut out circles of bread. Heat the clarified butter in a skillet until hot and fry the bread circles, browning on both sides. Drain on paper towels and set aside.
2. Rinse the turtle meat in cold water and drain. Put the turtle, stock and wine in a 3-quart saucepan. Bring to a boil, reduce heat to simmer and cook until the meat is tender—2 to 3 hours, depending on the size and age of the turtle.
3. Remove the meat from the liquid. Cool the meat and cut into bite-size pieces, removing all bones. Set aside.
4. Return the stock to heat, add the mushrooms and cook 5 minutes. Remove the mushrooms and set aside.
5. Over high heat, reduce the stock to about ½ cup. Add the sherry and cream and reduce to about ¼ cup. Remove from heat and add the unsalted butter in small pieces, whisking well until the butter is absorbed before adding more. Season with salt and freshly ground white pepper to taste.
6. Add the reserved meat and mushrooms and heat just barely to warm the meat through.
7. Place 1 piece of toast on each of 6 warm plates. Spoon the meat and sauce mixture over the toast, dividing evenly. Sprinkle with parsley and serve.

Note: The sauce can be made early in the day and gently reheated. It could be frozen before the addition of the egg and cream. The meat can be cooked early in the day and should be covered so it doesn't dry out. To reheat it, put it in a saucepan with a little sherry and heat quickly. Snapper turtles, also known as diamond-back turtles, can be bought whole, or the meat is available in bulk form at speciality food stores. The meat is comparable to the dark meat of chicken.

The secret to this appetizer is the Veal Stock. If you don't have any and don't care to make it at home, you can substitute Chicken Stock, but the superior quality of the appetizer will not be the same. I recommend canned chicken stock least. This dish is my own creation: I developed it after finding that turtle meat was available fresh locally.

Veal Stock

2 pounds veal bones
½ pound chicken backs and wings
2 carrots
2 ribs celery
1 medium-size onion
1 bay leaf
Pinch of thyme
6 parsley sprigs
1 leak, well cleaned
1 tomato
1 whole clove

1. Place the veal bones and chicken backs and wings in a stockpot and cover with cold water by 2″. Bring to a boil, reduce heat and simmer 1 hour. Pour off the water and discard; reserve bones.
2. Return the bones to the stockpot. Add the vegetables and cover with fresh cold water by 2″. Bring to a boil. Reduce heat to a bare simmer and cook 3 hours. Maintain the water level at 2″ above the ingredients. If it falls below that level, add more water.
3. Remove from heat and strain. Return the stock to the pot and simmer over medium heat until reduced by one-third.
4. Cool to room temperature, uncovered. Refrigerate overnight uncovered. Skim solidified fat from the top of the stock. Use stock as directed in recipe.

Note: This stock freezes well.

CREME DE MOULES
au Safran

¾ cup dry white wine
1 tablespoon finely chopped shallots
¼ cup finely chopped onion
¼ teaspoon saffron
2¼ cups bottled clam juice
4 pounds fresh mussels, scrubbed well in cold water, drained
4 egg yolks
1 cup whipping cream
Salt and freshly ground white pepper
Dash of cayenne pepper

1. Put the wine, shallots, onion and saffron in a 5-quart stainless steel pot and bring to a boil. Cook 5 minutes. Add the clam juice and return to boil.
2. Add the mussels, cover the pot and cook 5 to 6 minutes. Toss the mussels to bring those on the bottom of the pot to the surface. Cover the pot and cook 8 to 10 minutes over low heat.
3. Place a colander in a large pan and pour the contents of the pot into the colander. Reserve the mussels, discarding any that did not open. Strain the broth through a sieve lined with cheesecloth into a 2-quart stainless steel saucepan.
4. Bring the broth in the saucepan to a boil. Reduce the heat to simmer.
5. Combine the egg yolks and cream in a small bowl and whisk together. Add 1 cup broth to the eggs, whisking as liquid is added.
6. Pour the egg mixture into the remainder of the simmering broth, whisking gently. Return to a boil.
7. Remove from heat. Season with salt, pepper and cayenne pepper to taste.
8. Remove the mussels from their shells. Discard the shells. Place 5 to 6 mussels in each of 6 heated soup bowls. Pour the liquid over the mussels and serve at once.

Note: 4 pounds of mussels are necessary to make the broth for the soup. There will be cooked mussels left over and they can be combined with mayonnaise flavored with mustard to make an appetizer salad. Place the mixture on fresh lettuce and garnish with a tomato slice. The soup is also good served chilled. The broth can be prepared in advance through step 4.

The secret to the soup is to be sure that the mussels are well cleaned. If a mussel is particularly heavy, it is probably filled with mud. If you suspect that a mussel is mud-filled or is not fresh, try to pry it open. If it opens, it is not as fresh as it should be. Discard it.

In France this soup is known as Billy Bi. It was originated at Maxim's in Paris, where Chef Louis Barthe created it in 1950 for a regular customer, William Brand. He was called Billy Bi, and that's how the soup got its name. What I do is a takeoff on the original recipe. I make it with a stock made from turbot bones–the only way to get a fish stock that isn't "fishy". Unfortunately, turbot bones are rarely found in retail markets. The clam juice is an acceptable substitute; a light chicken broth would also serve.

SALADE GOURMANDE

2 small heads Boston lettuce
3 tablespoons walnut oil
1 tablespoon raspberry vinegar
Salt and freshly ground black pepper to taste
1 tablespoon finely chopped shallots
8 radishes, thinly sliced
½ cup thinly sliced mushrooms
½ cup finely shredded carrot

1. Discard the tough outer leaves of the lettuce. Cut large leaves in half lengthwise through the ribs, leaving small leaves whole. Wash several times in cold water, drain thoroughly and dry completely. Put in a plastic bag and chill in refrigerator.
2. Combine the oil, vinegar, salt and pepper in a salad bowl. Add the shallots. Mix well. Taste the dressing and add more salt and pepper if necessary.

3. Add the radishes, mushrooms and carrot. Mix. Add the lettuce and toss to coat with dressing.
4. Place on 6 chilled salad plates and serve immediately.

The essential ingredients in this recipe are the raspberry vinegar and the walnut oil. Shallot is an interesting ingredient that should not be omitted. Also, select very fresh lettuce and vegetables. Don't put the dressing on the salad too early or the vinegar will "burn" the lettuce, making it look and taste wilted. Serve the salad at the very beginning of the meal or just before dessert so the vinegar in the dressing will not clash with the wine.

GAMBETTES DE VOLAILLE
au Sauternes

¾ cup skinned and boned lean chicken meat
Salt
Freshly ground white pepper
Pinch of freshly grated nutmeg
¾ cup whipping cream
4 large chicken legs (including thigh), boned
Freshly ground black pepper
2 cups Chicken Stock (see index)
3 tablespoons Cognac
½ cup sauterne
4 tablespoons unsalted butter
Chopped fresh parsley for garnish

1. Place the chicken meat in the bowl of a food processor fitted with a steel blade. Coarsely chop the meat. Season with salt, white pepper and nutmeg.
2. With the machine running, slowly pour the cream through the feed tube. The mixture should be smooth and well-blended. Place in a bowl, cover with plastic wrap and chill.
3. Sprinkle the chicken leg cavity (from which the bones were removed) with salt and black pepper. Stuff with the chicken meat mixture, reconstructing as closely as possible the shape of the leg and thigh.
4. Wrap each stuffed leg in aluminum foil, twisting the ends to prevent stuffing from escaping.
5. Preheat oven to 180°.

6. Place the wrapped legs in a 2-quart stainless steel pot. Add the stock, Cognac and sauterne. Gradually bring to a boil. Cover, lower heat and simmer 15 minutes. Turn the wrapped legs over, recover pot and cook another 15 minutes. The legs should be just covered with liquid.
7. Remove the legs from the pot and place on a platter. Keep warm in preheated oven.
8. Reduce the liquid in the pot over medium-high heat to ¼ cup or until syrupy. Remove from heat and add the butter in small pieces, whisking vigorously. Add more butter only after the previous addition has been absorbed. Add any juices that have accumulated on the platter in the oven. Taste the sauce and add more salt and black pepper if needed.
9. Unwrap the chicken legs and place on a heated serving platter. Pour the sauce over and sprinkle with parsley. Service immediately.

Note: Assembled uncooked stuffed chicken legs can be frozen. Cooked chicken legs can be refrigerated in foil. To reheat, place in a preheated 300° oven 20 minutes. If preparing this dish ahead, let the wrapped cooked chicken legs cool in the cooking liquid before refrigerating. The sauce can be finished while the legs are reheating.

The secret to this recipe is not to overmix the chicken filling and to make it quickly so it does not have time to warm up. Overmixing and warming potentially could cause the filling to separate, ruining its texture. The beauty of this recipe is that even if you massacre the chicken legs when boning them, all is not lost. When you place the stuffing in the chicken and wrap it all in foil, mold it to look like a chicken leg. Reducing the cooking liquid as directed will concentrate flavors which will make a better-tasting sauce.

GRATIN DU SOLEIL

1 clove garlic, slightly crushed
Clarified butter
Flour
¾ pound zucchini, sliced ¼" thick
¾ pound eggplant, sliced ¼" thick, salted and dried of moisture
2 egg yolks
1 cup whipping cream
Salt
Freshly ground white pepper
Pinch of freshly grated nutmeg
¼ teaspoon dried oregano
¼ tablespoon dried basil
2 tablespoons grated Swiss cheese

1. Preheat oven to 400°. Butter a 12" oval gratin dish. Vigorously rub the garlic into the bottom of the dish. Discard garlic.
2. Lightly flour the eggplant slices and sauté with the zucchini slices in clarified butter. Arrange alternating layers of eggplant and zucchini in the dish.
3. Combine the yolks and cream in a bowl. Season with salt and pepper. Add the nutmeg, oregano and basil. Pour over the vegetables in the dish. Sprinkle with grated cheese.
4. Bake in preheated oven until tender and golden brown, about 15 minutes. Serve warm.

Note: This is good reheated. It can be assembled in advance and baked slightly to rewarm before serving.

Be especially careful not to overcook the custard. Fifteen minutes should be ample.

COUPE MERINGEE
aux Framboises

2 pints fresh raspberries
9 tablespoons sugar
¼ cup kirsch
1 cup whipping cream
1 teaspoon vanilla
4 **Meringue Shells**

1. Put half of the raspberries in a bowl. Sprinkle with 3 tablespoons sugar and the kirsch. Marinate 3 hours at room temperature, tossing once or twice.
2. Purée the remaining raspberries in a food processor or blender, adding 3 tablespoons sugar. Gently mix the puréed raspberries into the marinating raspberries.
3. Whip the cream to a soft consistency, gradually adding the remaining 3 tablespoons sugar. Add the vanilla and mix. The cream should not be too firm. Refrigerate until serving time.
4. To serve, coarsely crumble the **Meringue Shells** into a bowl. Fold in the whipped cream. Divide among 6 large glasses or bowls and top with the raspberry mixture. Serve immediately.

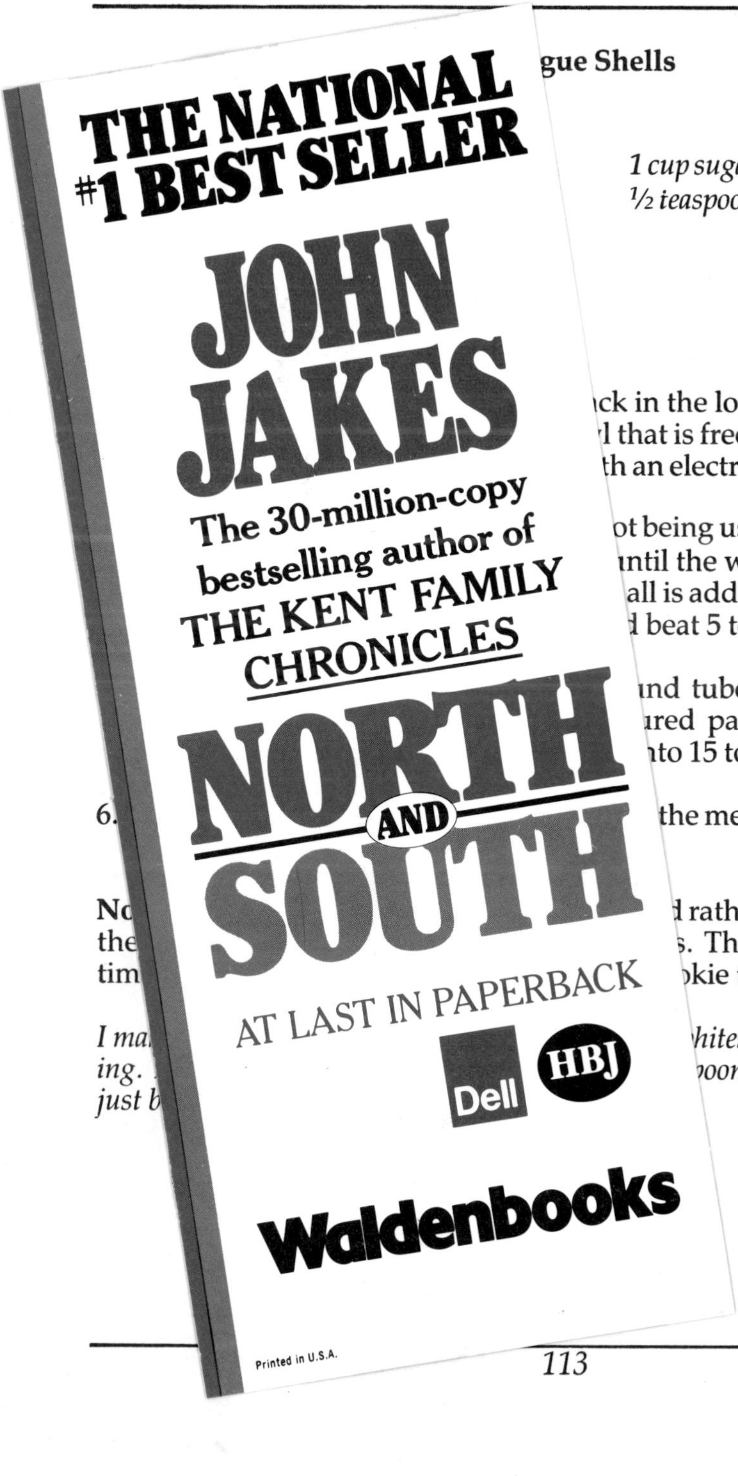

gue Shells

1 cup sugar
½ teaspoon vanilla

ick in the lower third of the oven.
l that is free of any grease or oil, or
th an electric mixer, beat at moder-

ot being used, the cream of tartar.
intil the whites hold soft peaks.
all is added. Add the vanilla and
l beat 5 to 7 minutes or until the

ind tube and fill half-full with
ired parchment paper or foil,
nto 15 to 18 shells. They will be

6. the meringues are very lightly

No l rather than trying to reduce
the s. The shells will last a long
tim okie tin.

I ma hites left over from other cook-
ing. oon the sauce over the cream
just b

JOHN ERNST CAFE

Dinner for Six

Liver Pâté

Beef Noodle Soup

Salad with Oil & Vinegar Dressing

Jäger Schnitzel

Spätzle

Mocha Torte

Wine:

With the Pâté—Ruppertsberger Linsenbusch Riesling, 1979
With the Schnitzel—Deidesheimer Herrgottsacker
Riesling, Kabinett, 1979

The Lindenberg Family, Proprietors
Dietmar Arnhold, Chef

JOHN ERNST CAFE

The John Ernst Cafe is rich in food history. Established in 1878, it is the city's oldest restaurant business continuously operating at the same address. For more than a century this address has been a center for *gemütlichkeit* and a favorite gathering place for many Milwaukeeans.

In 1878, Francis Krieg moved his saloon to what is now the John Ernst Cafe. Eight years later George M. Heiser took over the operation, with his wife serving food. Joseph Deutsch bought the place in 1922, renaming it the Ogden Cafe. It offered a complete menu until nine years later when Deutsch sold it to Paul Ezold and Arthur Poehnisch. In 1935, Deutsch reopened the restaurant as the Joe Deutsch Cafe and he hired John Ernst, a Hungarian immigrant, as a waiter.

In 1938, John Ernst bought the cafe from Deutsch and was associated with it until his death in 1980 at the age of eighty-one. Now his daughter Marianne and son-in-law Ervin Lindenberg own and manage the historic restaurant, where fine German food is a tradition. They are assisted by their two sons, John and Jim. There has been family involvement in the restaurant for more than forty years and all three generations have been active in it. "At every hour there is at least one family member on the premises. It's the only way to ensure quality," says Ervin Lindenberg.

Chef Dietmar Arnhold of Leipzig, Germany, heads the kitchen. His diverse culinary background and composure gives depth and unity to the cuisine. Arnhold began his cooking career in his father's bakery and worked in a variety of hotels and restaurants before joining the cafe eleven years ago.

The John Ernst Cafe is traditional in styling and the "booths" are some of the most popular in the city. Though called "booths" at the restaurant, they are more like small private dining rooms with four walls and doors. Many a business deal has been struck here throughout the years. For romantics, the Rhine Room with its massive natural fireplace is a must on a snowy winter night.

600 East Ogden Avenue

LIVER PATE

¾ pound Spanish onions, chopped
⅓ cup rendered duck or chicken fat
¾ pound fresh chicken or duck livers, washed and drained
⅛ teaspoon dried marjoram
⅛ teaspoon dried sweet basil
¼ teaspoon salt
Freshly ground black pepper
Crackers

1. Sauté the onions in the fat in a large sauté pan until translucent, but not brown.
2. Add the livers and sauté until cooked through, stirring constantly. While hot, drain all the fat from the pan. Sprinkle with the marjoram and basil.
3. Put the sautéed mixture through a meat grinder, or process in a food processor, until smooth. Add salt and pepper to taste.
4. Spoon into a serving dish and chill. Serve slightly chilled with your choice of crackers.

Note: Pâté must be made ahead and will keep for 4 days if covered tightly and refrigerated.

It is important to thoroughly drain off all of the fat from the pan before grinding the meat.

BEEF NOODLE SOUP

2 to 2½ pounds beef bones, cracked
½ gallon plus ¼ cup water
1 large onion, quartered
1 medium-size carrot, coarsely chopped
1 medium-size parsnip, coarsely chopped, with ¼ cup stems and leaves
1 to 2 ribs celery, coarsely chopped
1 tomato, coarsely chopped
1 tablespoon beef bouillon granules
¼ teaspoon whole black peppercorns
Noodles

1. Preheat oven to 450°.
2. Place the bones in a roasting pan and brown in preheated oven for 30 minutes or until nut brown.
3. Add ¼ cup water to the pan while hot and scape the crusty bits from the bottom of the pan. Pour the water and bones into a stockpot.
4. Add the remaining ingredients except the **Noodles,** bring to a boil, reduce heat and simmer 5 hours uncovered.
5. Strain the stock through a sieve lined with damp white cotton cloth or a coffee filter.
6. When cold, remove the layer of fat from the top of the stock. Bring to a simmer and add **Noodles.** Heat through and serve immediately.

When making the beef stock, be sure to brown the bones well, but take care not to burn them.

Noodles

1½ teaspoons salt
3 cups hot water
1½ cups fine egg noodles

1. Put the salt and water in a large kettle and bring to a rolling boil.
2. Add the noodles and allow to boil slowly 5 to 8 minutes.
3. Remove from heat and drain in a colander. Hold the colander under cold running water to stop cooking, remove excess starch and prevent the noodles from clinging together.

Note: The beef stock must be made in advance. It can be frozen. If desired, the noodles can be prepared the day before serving, and refrigerated. The procedure for cooking the noodles can be used in numerous recipes when precooked noodles or pasta are desired. To reheat, place the cold noodles or pasta in a sieve and submerge in hot water.

SALAD WITH OIL AND VINEGAR DRESSING

1 large head iceberg lettuce, cleaned, dried, chilled and broken into bite-size pieces
2 ripe tomatoes, cored and cut into wedges
½ small cucumber, thinly sliced
Oil and Vinegar Dressing

Place the lettuce, tomato wedges and cucumber slices in a large salad bowl. Drizzle with dressing, tossing to coat the leaves and vegetables. Serve immediately.

Oil and Vinegar Dressing

½ cup salad oil
¾ cup white vinegar
½ cup water
¾ teaspoon salt
Freshly ground black pepper to taste
¾ teaspoon sugar

Mix all ingredients to blend thoroughly.

Note: Extra dressing keeps indefinitely in a covered jar in the refrigerator.

Be sure to shake the dressing well before using.

JÄGER SCHNITZEL

3 pounds premium veal tenderloin
Salt
Paprika
Flour
3 ounces clarified butter
Mushroom Sauce
Chopped fresh parsley

1. Slice the veal into 12 slices (about ¼ pound each). Pound flat with the side of a cleaver. Sprinkle each cutlet with salt and paprika and dredge in flour.
2. Preheat oven to 200°.
3. Sauté the cutlets in the clarified butter until cooked through and golden brown, about 2 to 3 minutes on each side, over medium-high heat. Do not overcook. Hold the sautéed cutlets in preheated oven until all are sautéed.
4. Place 2 cutlets on each of 6 plates and pour ½ cup **Mushroom Sauce** over each serving. Sprinkle with chopped parsley and serve immediately.

Note: The sauce can be made in advance, but the veal cannot be cooked until serving time.

Veal inside round steak, sliced across the grain, may be substituted for the tenderloin.

When browning the veal cutlets, it is important that the pan be hot before the veal goes in, but not so hot that it burns the butter.

Mushroom Sauce

½ to ¾ cup finely minced shallots
2 ounces clarified butter
⅓ cup all-purpose flour
1½ tablespoons tomato purée
3½ cups VEAL STOCK
1 pound mushrooms, cleaned and halved
1 cup Chablis
½ teaspoon salt

1. Sauté the shallots in the butter in a 4-quart saucepan until translucent.
2. Add the flour, stirring constantly with a whisk. Cook 4 to 5 minutes, but don't brown.
3. Add the tomato purée and whisk to combine. Slowly add 1¾ cups **Veal Stock** and whisk to combine. Add the remaining stock and stir to blend. Bring to a boil and reduce heat to simmer.
4. Add the mushrooms, Chablis and salt. Simmer 5 to 10 minutes and serve immediately.

VEAL STOCK

2 to 2½ pounds veal bones, cracked
½ gallon plus ½ cup water
1 large onion, quartered
1 medium-size carrot, coarsely chopped
1 medium-size parsnip, coarsely chopped, with about ¼ cup stems and leaves
1 to 2 ribs celery, coarsely chopped
1 tomato, coarsely chopped
1 tablespoon beef bouillon granules
¼ teaspoon whole black peppercorns

1. Preheat oven to 450°.
2. Place the bones in a roasting pan and brown in preheated oven for 30 minutes or until nut brown.
3. Add ½ cup water to the pan while hot and scrape the crusty bits from the pan bottom. Pour the water and the bones into a stockpot.
4. Add the remaining ingredients, bring to a boil, reduce heat and simmer 5 hours uncovered.
5. Strain the stock through a sieve lined with a damp white cotton cloth or a coffee filter. Allow to cool to room temperature. Refrigerate overnight.
6. When cold, remove the solidified fat from the top of the stock. Bring the stock to a boil, reduce heat and simmer 1 hour before using.

Note: Extra Veal Stock can be frozen. The sauce can be made in advance, but the veal cannot be cooked until serving time.

SPÄTZLE

2 tablespoons salt
4 eggs
½ cup cold water
3 cups all-purpose flour
Butter (optional)

1. Fill a 4 to 6-quart pot two-thirds full of water and add the salt. Bring to a rolling boil.
2. To make the batter, combine the eggs and cold water with a whisk. Add the flour 1 cup at a time, blending each cup thoroughly with a wooden spoon.
3. If you have a spätzle mill, mill the batter into the rapidly boiling salted water. If not, place the batter in a strong plastic bag. Snip one corner of the bag, forming a hole the diameter of a pencil. Carefully squeeze the batter into the boiling water through the bag.
4. Bring the water to a boil. Simmer 1 minute.
5. Drain into a colander and serve immediately with butter if desired.

Note: Spätzle can be made in advance through step 4. Drain into a colander, rinse under cold water until cold to the touch and refrigerate. To reheat, place in a colander and set the colander under hot running water or in a kettle of hot water until heated through, about 2 minutes.

It is important that the water be at a rolling boil when the batter goes in.

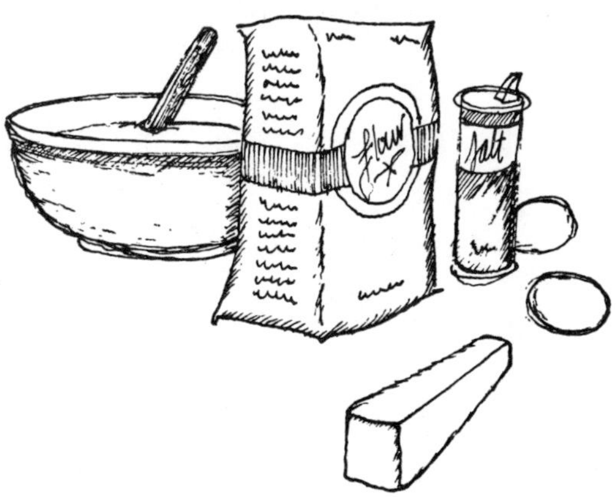

MOCHA TORTE

6 eggs, separated, room temperature
1 tablespoon plus 1 teaspoon cold water
½ teaspoon salt
1½ teaspoons vanilla
1 cup super-fine sugar
1 cup cake flour, unsifted
1 teaspoon baking powder
Frosting

1. Preheat oven to 375°.
2. Combine the egg yolks, cold water, salt and vanilla in a mixing bowl. Whisk until smooth. Set aside.
3. Beat the egg whites in a large bowl until soft peaks form. Slowly add the sugar while beating and mix well.
4. Slowly add the yolk mixture to the whites, mixing on low speed until the yolks are thoroughly blended in.
5. Sift the flour and baking powder together and add to the egg mixture with the mixer on its slowest speed. Do not overmix. Divide the batter between 2 greased and floured 9" round cake pans. Bake in preheated oven 30 minutes or until the tops are almond brown.
6. Invert the layers onto wax paper and cool on racks. When cool, slice each into 3 horizontal layers, making a total of 6 layers. Discard the wax paper.
7. Place 1 layer on a serving plate and spread with **Frosting**. Repeat, stacking the layers. When all the layers are in place, the torte is completed. Top and sides may be frosted if desired.

Frosting

1 pound unsalted butter, room temperature
1 egg yolk, room temperature
½ pound powdered sugar
3½ ounces very strong black coffee, cold

1. Cream the butter in a mixing bowl with the egg yolk until nearly white in color.
2. Slowly add the sugar and coffee alternately, ending with sugar.

It is important that the egg yolk and butter are at room temperature.

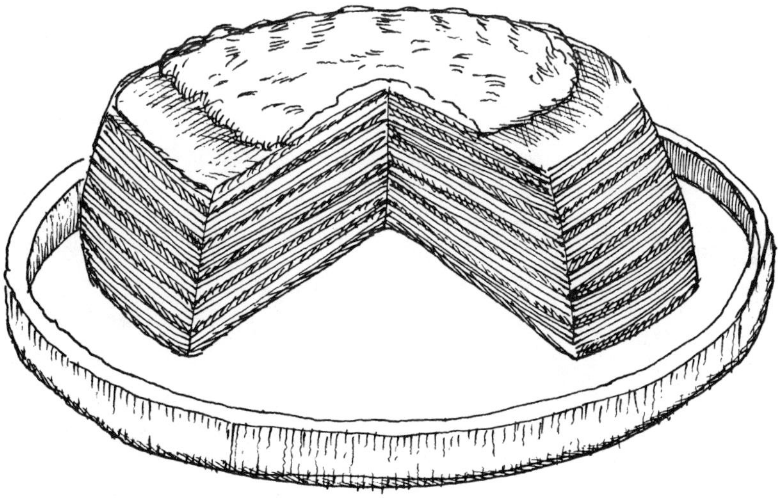

Karl Ratzsch's

Dinner for Four

Stuffed Mushroom Caps

Ratzsch's Bean Soup

Spinach Salad with Hot Bacon Dressing

Roast Goose Shanks

Burgundy Red Cabbage

Mocha Torte

Wine:

With the Mushrooms–Ayler Kupp Kabinett, 1976
With the Goose–Clos de Vougeot, 1970

The Karl Ratzsch Family, Proprietors
Michael Dreazy, Chef

KARL RATZSCH'S

Karl Ratzsch's is well-known in Milwaukee for its German food and old-world atmosphere. It is the recipient of numerous awards for fine food and service, most notably the *Travel/Holiday* Award every year since 1952. Ratzsch's also is unique for its collection of German artifacts and antiques which decorates the dining rooms. A string trio adds music to the comfortable surroundings.

Like many of Milwaukee's fine restaurants, Ratzsch's is family owned and operated. In 1929, Karl and Helen Ratzsch founded the restaurant. Being a good cook, Mrs. Ratzsch liked the restaurant business because of the people. She cooked in the restaurant for years until retirement, and many of her recipes are still used today. Karl Ratzsch, Jr. carried on the tradition. He was schooled in restaurant management at Cornell University. Now, a member of the third generation, Karl Ratzsch III, acts as general manager, overseeing day-to-day operations at the restaurant.

Michael Dreazy is executive chef, supervising the large kitchen staff. He worked in many Milwaukee restaurants and private clubs before joining Ratzsch's, including the Simon House, the old Frenchy's, Eugene's and the University Club.

A good chef, in Ratzsch's opinion, is one who puts in many hours, frequently "has his finger in the pot" and handles the restaurant personnel well. "I always look for someone who is willing to get in the kitchen and cook," adds Karl Ratzsch III.

Popular items at Ratzsch's include Sauerbraten, Roast Goose Shanks, Baked Pork Shank, Liver Dumpling Soup, Spinach with Hot Bacon Dressing and Bratwurst and Smoked Pork Chops served with sauerkraut, potato dumplings and purée of peas.

320 East Mason Street

STUFFED MUSHROOM CAPS

3 cups fresh mushrooms, about 1" diameter, washed and dried
4 tablespoons butter
2 tablespoons finely chopped celery
2 tablespoons finely chopped onion
Pinch of salt
Pinch of freshly ground black pepper
Pinch of freshly grated nutmeg
Pinch of sage
1 cup ground cooked chicken meat
1 egg, beaten
¼ cup dry bread crumbs
4 slices toast

1. Remove the mushroom stems from the caps, reserving the caps. Chop the stems very finely and sauté in 2 tablespoons butter in a sauté pan with the celery, onion, salt, pepper, nutmeg and sage. Cool.
2. Blend the ground chicken and the egg with the sautéed mixture. Add the bread crumbs gradually until the chicken mixture takes on a doughy consistency. If the mixture becomes too dry, add more butter until the consistency is moldable.
3. Stuff the chicken mixture into the mushroom caps.
4. Sauté the filled mushroom caps in 2 tablespoons butter in a sauté pan over medium heat for 10 to 15 minutes or until the caps are cooked and the filling is heated through.
5. Drain the filled mushrooms on paper towels and divide over 4 slices of toast. Serve while hot.

Note: This recipe can be prepared in advance through step 3, covering the filled mushroom caps and refrigerating them until about 1 hour before cooking time. Bring to room temperature and cook just before serving for best results.

RATZSCH'S BEAN SOUP

2 pounds smoked pork loin, or 3 pounds smoked ham shanks
1 cup chopped onion
1 cup chopped celery
1 cup chopped carrots
1 tablespoon chicken soup base, or 3 cubes chicken bouillon
1 teaspoon Accent
1 pound tomatoes, peeled and chopped
1 cup dry navy beans, soaked overnight
½ teaspoon freshly ground black pepper
2 teaspoons salt
1 tablespoon beef soup base, or 3 cubes beef bouillon
Roux
Croutons
Chopped fresh parsley

1. Place the smoked meat in a soup kettle with 1 gallon water and boil until tender, about 45 to 60 minutes. Remove the meat, dice and set aside. Put 2 quarts of this stock in a large saucepan.
2. Add the onion, celery, carrots, chicken base or bouillon cubes, Accent, tomatoes, beans, pepper, salt and beef base or bouillon to the saucepan with the stock. Cook over medium-high heat until the beans are tender, from 1 to 3 hours. If more liquid is needed, use the remaining stock.
3. Add the reserved diced meat to the soup. Return to a boil and thicken with **Roux**. Cook 5 minutes longer, stirring frequently.
4. Ladle into bowls and garnish with croutons and chopped parsley.

Note: This soup freezes well, but the garnish should not be added until just before serving time.

Roux

4 tablespoons butter
4 tablespoons flour

Melt the butter in a sauté pan over medium-high heat. When the butter sizzles, add the flour all at once. Cook, stirring constantly, 3 to 4 minutes until the mixture is a smooth paste.

SPINACH SALAD
with Hot Bacon Dressing

½ pound bacon, diced
1 large white onion, diced
½ cup white vinegar
1 teaspoon salt
½ teaspoon freshly gound black pepper
1 to 2 teaspoons sugar
2 tablespoons cornstarch
1 cup chicken consommé
1 pound fresh spinach, cleaned, stemmed and dried

1. Sauté the bacon until crisp. Drain and set aside.
2. Sauté the onion in the bacon drippings until translucent. Add the vinegar, salt, pepper and sugar.
3. Dissolve the cornstarch in the consommé and add to the sautéed mixture, stirring until slightly thickened. Cook over medium heat. Return the cooked diced bacon to the dressing.
4. Divide the spinach among 4 salad plates and pour the hot dressing over. Serve immediately.

Note: Be sure not to scorch the dressing while cooking it. The dressing can be adjusted by adding more vinegar for a more tart taste, or by adding more sugar for a sweeter taste.

ROAST GOOSE SHANKS

1 tablespoon shortening
4 (14 to 16-ounce) goose shanks
Salt and freshly ground black pepper
2 apples, peeled, quartered, and cored
2 medium-size onions, chopped
1 quart hot Chicken Stock (see index)
¼ cup flour
⅓ dry red wine

1. Preheat oven to 350°.
2. Put the shortening in a roasting pan large enough to hold the goose shanks. Place the pan in preheated oven to melt the shortening.
3. Sprinkle the shanks with salt and pepper. Place fat-side-down in the hot roasting pan and bake 30 minutes or until browned. Drain off and reserve fat during roasting.
4. Add the apples, onions, chicken stock, ½ teaspoon salt, and ¼ teaspoon pepper to the roasting pan and bake another 90 minutes or until the shanks are tender. Every 20 minutes, skim the accumulated fat from the surface of the liquid.
5. Remove the shanks from the pan and place on a warm platter. Set the roasting pan on the stove.
6. Place ¼ cup reserved goose fat in a small saucepan. Add the flour and cook over high heat, stirring constantly, 2 to 3 minutes.
7. Heat the drippings in the roasting pan and stir the goose fat/flour mixture into the hot drippings, stirring until thickened. Stir in the wine and cook 2 to 3 minutes more. Strain the sauce and serve over the roasted goose shanks.

Note: This entrée can be prepared completely in advance. Put the roasted goose shanks in the sauce in a roasting pan, cover and refrigerate. To reheat, put the covered pan in a preheated 300° oven for 20 to 30 minutes or until the goose is hot throughout.

Goose gives off a lot of fat during roasting. This fat should be drained off or skimmed. There are uses for goose fat; it can be added to vegetables from the cabbage family for added flavor or it can be spread on bread like butter.

BURGUNDY RED CABBAGE

1 small head cabbage, coarsely sliced
1 apple, peeled, cored, and finely chopped
1 small onion, finely chopped
1 tablespoon salt
1/4 cup sugar
3/4 cup red wine vinegar
1 cup water
1 cup dry red wine
4 strips bacon, minced and cooked
1/4 teaspoon mustard seed
1/4 teaspoon dill seed
1/4 teaspoon dried red pepper flakes
4 whole cloves
1 bay leaf

Place all the ingredients in a large kettle and boil until tender, about 20 to 30 minutes. The mixture should not be too mushy or it will take on a blue cast.

Note: Be careful not to overcook the cabbage. There will be some liquid in the finished dish. It should not be cooked to the point of dryness.

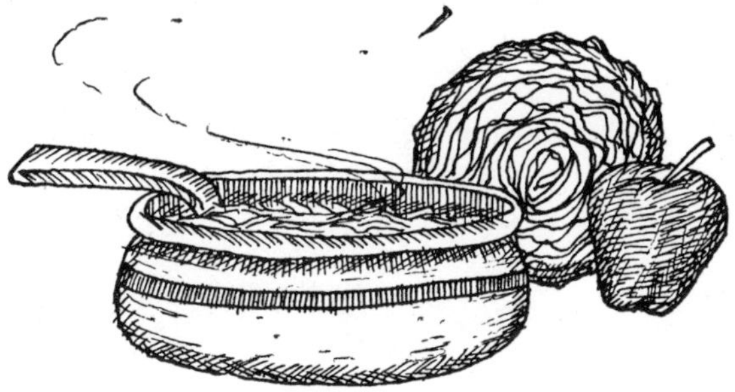

MOCHA TORTE

7 eggs
1 cup sugar
1½ cups ground walnuts
½ cup dry bread crumbs
3 tablespoons light rum
3 tablespoons dark rum
Chocolate Butter Cream Frosting

1. Separate 6 eggs. Beat the whole egg, separated yolks and ¾ cup sugar in a large mixing bowl until very creamy and light.
2. Preheat oven to 350°.
3. In another large bowl, beat the egg whites with ¼ cup sugar until the whites hold stiff peaks. Do not overbeat the whites until they are dry.
4. Fold the egg yolk mixture, alternating with the walnuts and bread crumbs, into the beaten whites.
5. Divide the batter among 3 (8") buttered and floured round cake pans. Bake in preheated oven 25 minutes.
6. Remove the pans from the oven and cool on racks. When cool, remove the layers from the pans. Cut each layer in half horizontally. Mix the rums together and sprinkle each layer with the rum mixture.
7. Place one layer on a serving plate and cover thinly with **Chocolate Butter Cream Frosting**. Cover with another layer and frost, continuing until the torte is assembled. Frost the entire outside of the torte.

When making the torte, be gentle when folding the two mixtures together so that the air in the egg whites is not eliminated during the folding process.

Chocolate Butter Cream Frosting

½ cup unsalted butter
2 ounces semisweet chocolate, melted and cooled
1 egg yolk
½ cup powdered sugar
1 teaspoon rum

1. Cream the butter in a large bowl until fluffy. Gradually beat in the chocolate.
2. In another bowl, beat the egg yolk and sugar until creamy.
3. Beat the egg/sugar mixture into the chocolate mixture until very light and smooth.
4. Add the rum and mix.

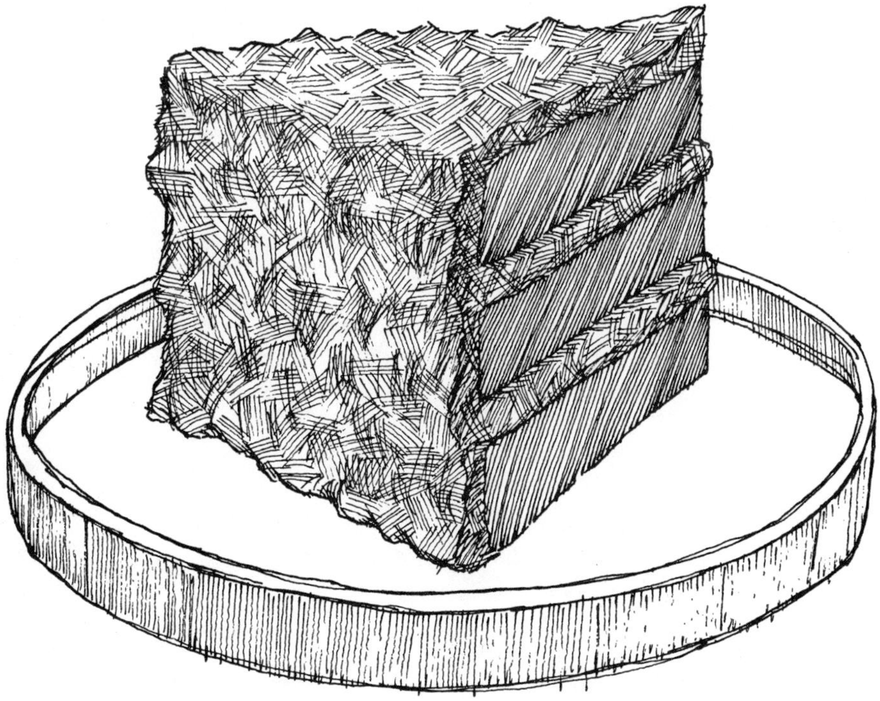

Dinner for Six

Spinach Pie

Avgolemono Soup

Greek Salad

Lamb Shish Kebabs

Rice

Baklava

Wine:
Roditis

Kostas Demopoulos, Proprietor and Chef

KOSTA'S WHITE MANOR INN

Kosta's White Manor Inn is a delightfully cozy place on a hill overlooking Lake Michigan. It is well known throughout Milwaukee for its fine Greek food; the Spinach Pie, Greek Salad and Baklava are just a few of the favorites here. Chef and proprietor Kostas Demopoulos cooks like chefs do in the old country—by touch. But he did take time to convert his technique of cooking by touch to written recipes for this book.

Demopoulos came to America in 1960 and worked in his uncles' nightclub and restaurant in Tomahawk, Wisconsin, for seven years. He knows his way around a kitchen and is expert in the Greek cuisine, having served his chef's apprenticeship in Athens beginning in 1950 and working as a chef in Greece before coming to America.

Only the best ingredients are used by Chef Demopoulos, who cooks everything from scratch on the premises of his small restaurant every day. Tables are small and intimate, illuminated by candles whose light is caught in the stucco arches. Bay windows are filled with plants that allow the morning sun to filter through. The air is deliciously scented with the smell of homemade bread.

1234 East Juneau Avenue

SPINACH PIE

3 pounds fresh spinach
1½ cups olive oil
1 medium-size onion, finely chopped
1 bunch scallions, finely chopped
1½ tablespoons flour
1 tablespoon chopped fresh dill, or 1 teaspoon dried dill
¼ teaspoon freshly grated nutmeg
½ teaspoon freshly ground white pepper
¼ cup grated Parmesan cheese
5 eggs, lightly beaten
1½ pounds feta cheese, crumbled
1 (1-pound) package frozen phyllo dough, thawed in wrappings
Melted butter

1. Thoroughly wash the spinach, remove the stems and wring completely dry. Chop coarsely.
2. Preheat oven to 350°.
3. Put the oil in a very large sauté pan and heat. When hot, add the onion and scallions. Sauté until translucent. Add the spinach and sauté until the oil is absorbed and the spinach is almost dry. Add the flour and sauté 1 to 2 minutes. Remove from heat.
4. Add the dill, nutmeg, white pepper and Parmesan cheese. Stir to mix. Add the eggs and feta cheese and mix.
5. Lay a sheet of phyllo dough on the work surface and brush with melted butter. Top with a second and third sheet, brushing each with butter. Place one-sixth of the spinach mixture in the center of the dough and wrap to contain the filling. Brush with melted butter and place on a baking sheet. Make 5 more pieces in the same manner.
6. Bake in preheated oven 20 to 25 minutes. Serve immediately.

Note: These can be made in advance through step 5. Wrap lightly with plastic wrap and refrigerate. Remove from the refrigerator 15 minutes before baking. Baked Spinach Pies can be reheated in a 350° oven 10 minutes. Unbaked Spinach Pies can be frozen if tightly wrapped.

When working with phyllo dough, follow the directions on the package. The dough is fragile and dries quickly so don't remove dough from package until you are ready to work with it. Don't worry if it tears.

AVGOLEMONO SOUP

5 cups Chicken Stock (see index)
1/4 cup raw rice, washed in cold water
4 egg yolks, lightly beaten
4 teaspoons flour
Juice of 1 1/2 lemons
1 1/2 teaspoons salt
Pinch of ground white pepper

1. Place the Chicken Stock in a 2-quart saucepan and bring to a boil. Add the rice, return to a boil, cover, reduce heat and cook 10 minutes. Remove from heat; set aside, but keep warm.
2. Put 1 cup cold water in a 2-quart saucepan. Whisking continuously, add the egg yolks and flour.
3. Heat and gradually add the chicken stock/rice mixture, whisking continuously. Add the lemon juice, salt and pepper. Heat through and serve immediately.

GREEK SALAD

1 small head iceberg lettuce, cleaned, wrung completely dry and julienned
1 head endive, cleaned and dried, julienned
1 small head romaine lettuce, cleaned and dried, julienned
1/2 green pepper, julienned
1 bunch watercress, cleaned and dried, large stems removed, chopped
1/4 pound fresh spinach, cleaned and dried, stems removed, chopped
1 small cucumber, partially peeled, thinly sliced, or 1 large onion, thinly sliced
1 bunch scallions, white part only, chopped
1 tablespoon chopped fresh dill
1 cup olive oil
1/3 cup cider vinegar
Sprinkling of ground white pepper
1 teaspoon dried oregano
1 pound feta cheese, crumbled
12 flat anchovy filets, well drained
24 to 30 salted Greek olives
12 thin slices tomato

1. Place the iceberg, endive, romaine, green pepper, watercress, spinach, cucumber, scallions and dill in a large salad bowl.
2. In a small bowl, whisk together the oil and vinegar. Add the white pepper and oregano and mix.
3. Pour the oil mixture over the greens and toss to combine. Divide the salad mixture among 6 salad plates. Garnish each plate with one-sixth of the cheese, 2 anchovy filets, 4 to 5 olives and 2 slices tomato. Serve immediately.

Note: The ingredients in step 1 can be assembled in a bowl, covered with plastic wrap and refrigerated several hours before serving. The dressing can be made ahead of time and reserved at room temperature. Step 3 should be completed just prior to serving the salad.

Omit the dill if it can't be found fresh.

LAMB SHISH KEBABS

4¼ pounds prime leg of lamb, cubed 1" by 2", excess fat trimmed
2 green peppers, cut 1" by 2"
1 onion, cut 1" by 2"
2 tomatoes, each cut into 6 wedges
12 mushrooms
6 bay leaves
½ cup olive oil
1 cup dry sherry
1 teaspoon dried oregano
Pinch of salt
Pinch of freshly ground black pepper

1. Assemble 6 skewers so that each contains about 10 ounces of lamb, one-sixth each of the green pepper and onion pieces, 2 tomato wedges, 2 mushrooms and 1 bay leaf. Alternate chunks of meat with vegetables in an attractive manner. Put the bay leaf in the center of each skewer. Place all completed skewers in the bottom of a flat pan.
2. Combine the oil, sherry, oregano, salt and pepper and pour over the kebabs. Turn the kebabs to coat well. Marinate at least 30 minutes at room temperature, or as long as overnight, covered and refrigerated.

(continued next page)

3. Bring the kebabs to room temperature if they have been refrigerated. Preheat broiler to hot. Remove the kebabs from the marinade and broil about 10 minutes, turning after 5 minutes, to medium doneness. Serve immediately.

Note: Lamb Shish Kebabs can be prepared in advance through step 2.

RICE

4 cups Chicken Stock (see index)
½ cup butter
2 cups rice, washed in cold water
1 tablespoon salt
Sprinkling of ground white pepper
Juice of ½ lemon

1. Preheat oven to 350°.
2. Place the stock and butter in a large saucepan. Bring to a boil.
3. Add the rice, salt, pepper and lemon juice. Return to a boil and cover.
4. Bake 25 minutes in preheated oven. Serve hot with **Shish Kebabs**.

Note: The rice can be prepared early on the day it is to be served and reheated in a microwave oven. Allow 1 minute on high power for each cup of rice.

BAKLAVA

1 pound walnuts, coarsely chopped, lightly toasted
½ pound almonds, coarsely chopped, lightly toasted
½ teaspoon ground cinnamon
¼ teaspoon vanilla
1½ pounds butter, melted
1 (1-pound) package frozen phyllo dough, thawed in wrappings
2 cups sugar
1 cup water
Pinch of salt
1 lemon
1 stick cinnamon
6 whole cloves
1 cup honey

1. In a bowl, mix the walnuts, almonds, cinnamon, vanilla and 1 tablespoon melted butter. Set aside.
2. Brush a 9" by 12" baking pan with some melted butter and place 1 sheet of phyllo dough in the pan. Brush with the melted butter. Continue in this manner until 8 sheets of dough are in the pan, brushing melted butter between each sheet of dough.
3. Alternate the filling with all but 6 sheets of the remaining phyllo dough, brushing each sheet of dough with melted butter.
4. Top with 6 sheets phyllo dough, one at a time, brushing melted butter between each sheet. Cut the baklava into triangles or squares.
5. Bake in preheated 300° oven 2 hours. Remove from oven and cool completely.
6. Place the sugar and water in a saucepan and bring to a boil. Add the salt, juice and rind of the lemon, cinnamon stick and cloves. Return to a boil. Remove from heat, strain and stir in the honey. Immediately pour over cold baklava while the syrup is hot.

Note: The Baklava should be made in advance and served at room temperature.

Mader's

Dinner for Six

Koenigsberger Klops

Chicken Broth with Spätzle

Cucumber Salad

Sauerbraten with Potato Dumplings

Apple Sauerkraut

Apple Cake

Wine:

With the Sauerbraten–Eltviller Sonnenberg Spätlese
With the Cake–Siebeldinger Koenigsberg Auslese

Gustave and Victor Mader, Proprietors
Gerry Schoenig, Chef

MADER'S

In 1902, an ambitious young German immigrant named Charles Mader bought a small building at 233 West Water St. (now Plankinton Avenue). He called it the Comfort because of its clean wooden floors, "soft" wooden chairs and oak tables. The restaurant's present $100,000 collection of medieval Germanic weaponry was not yet on display, but the Comfort fared well. It has moved to its present location after a short time.

After eighteen years of successful operation, the restaurant was faced with Prohibition in 1919, and Mader focused all of his attention on his kitchen and the rustic German dishes he knew. Sauerbraten, Wienerschnitzel and Pork Shank kept patrons coming back even though they couldn't again enjoy them with a stein of beer until 1933.

Mader's sons, George and Gustave, helped their father in the restaurant until the elder Mader died in 1937. Then Gus and George continued to operate the restaurant, adding the Jaeger Stube to the establishment in 1952 to celebrate the restaurant's fiftieth year of operation. When George died in 1958, Gus took over Mader's, succeeding in maintaining this fine restaurant where *gemütlichkeit* is still the byword.

In 1964, Gus's son Victor entered the family business after studying hotel and restaurant management at Michigan State University and in Switzerland and southern Germany. With Victor sharing in the management responsibilities, Gus was enabled to spend more time traveling through Europe, discovering recipes for the Continent's well-known foods. The menu at Mader's changes to reflect recipes that Gus collects on his travels. Mader has also introduced four new German wines, bottled under his own label, at his restaurant where the wine list displays 200 fine vintages. To celebrate the restaurant's seventy-fifth anniversary, Mader added a Rhein Stube which seats one hundred and is frequently used for special parties.

Chef Gerry Schoenig takes advantage of seasonal foods, featuring them in the extensive menu of German specialties. Schoenig began his professional training at the age of fourteen in Neustadt and later worked in Baden-Baden. He brings the European philosophy of cuisine and kitchen management to Mader's.

1041 North Third Street

KOENIGSBERGER KLOPS

¾ pound lean beef
¼ pound lean pork
½ pound lean veal
1 medium-size onion, minced (approximately ½ cup)
3 tablespoons butter
1 cup dry bread crumbs
2 eggs, beaten
1¾ teaspoons salt
¼ teaspoon freshly ground black pepper
3 cups water
1 bay leaf
1 whole clove
3 black peppercorns
½ onion, sliced
2 tablespoons flour
2 tablespoons lemon juice, or 1 tablespoon capers
1 cup dry Rhine wine

1. Grind the beef, pork and veal together twice. Place in a bowl.
2. Sauté the minced onion in 1 tablespoon butter until translucent, not brown. Add to the meats in the bowl.
3. Add the bread crumbs, eggs, 1½ teaspoons salt and ground pepper to the meats and stir only until blended. Form into 1½" to 2" meatballs.
4. Bring the water to a boil in a large kettle with the bay leaf, clove, peppercorns, sliced onion and ¼ teaspoon salt.
5. Add the meatballs and simmer gently 30 minutes or until done. Remove the meatballs with a slotted spoon and keep warm. Strain the cooking liquid and reserve.
6. Melt 2 tablespoons butter in a saucepan over medium-high heat. When bubbling, stir in the flour and cook 2 minutes.
7. Gradually add 1 cup reserved cooking liquid, cooking and stirring until smooth and thickened.
8. Add the remaining cooking liquid and the lemon juice or capers.
9. Return the meatballs to the sauce and heat to serving temperature. Remove from heat and gently stir in the wine. Serve immediately.

Note: This appetizer can be made in advance and served hot or cold. Reheat the meatballs slowly in the sauce.

Be sure to stir the wine into the sauce off the heat or the mixture will curdle.

CHICKEN BROTH WITH SPÄTZLE

1 (5 to 6-pound) stewing fowl, disjointed
3 quarts water
¼ cup chopped celery tops
1 stalk celery, chopped
¼ cup sliced carrot
¼ cup diced onion
3 black peppercorns
1 teaspoon salt
Spätzle

1. Arrange the chicken pieces in a large kettle. Add the water and bring to a boil.
2. Skim surface occasionally to remove scum.
3. Add the celery tops, celery, carrot, onion, peppercorns and salt. Cover the kettle and simmer gently 2½ to 3 hours.
4. Remove the less-meaty pieces of chicken as they become tender; set aside. When the meatiest pieces of chicken are tender, remove them from the broth. (Reserve cooked chicken for casseroles or salads.)
5. Strain the broth and cool at room temperature. When cool, refrigerate uncovered.
6. Remove solidified fat from the surface of the broth.
7. Bring the broth to a boil and drop in **Spätzle** by teaspoonfuls.
8. Simmer gently about 10 minutes. Serve immediately.

Note: This soup can be made in advance and gently reheated.

Spätzle

1 egg
½ teaspoon salt
½ cup water
¾ cup sifted flour
Pinch of freshly grated nutmeg
½ teaspoon yellow food coloring

1. Beat the egg with the salt and combine with the water. Add the flour, nutmeg and food coloring and stir to a smooth batter.
2. Beat 5 to 8 minutes or until the mixture is fluffy. Use as directed in soup.

CUCUMBER SALAD

1 long, slender cucumber
1 teaspoon salt
3 tablespoons white vinegar
1 tablespoon sugar
Pinch of freshly ground white pepper
1 green onion, finely sliced, including green top
½ cup sour cream
2 tablespoons finely minced parsley

1. If the cucumber is not tender or if it has been waxed, peel and score lengthwise with fork. Slice very thinly. Sprinkle with salt, put in a bowl and refrigerate.
2. In another bowl, mix the vinegar with the sugar, pepper and onion. Stir in the sour cream.
3. Press the moisture from the cucumber slices, draining very thoroughly.
4. Add the dressing to the cucumber slices. Mix well and transfer to a small serving bowl. Garnish with parsley. Chill. Serve cold.

Note: This salad can be made in advance. Keep it refrigerated.

The secret to this salad is thoroughly drying the cucumber slices before adding them to the dressing.

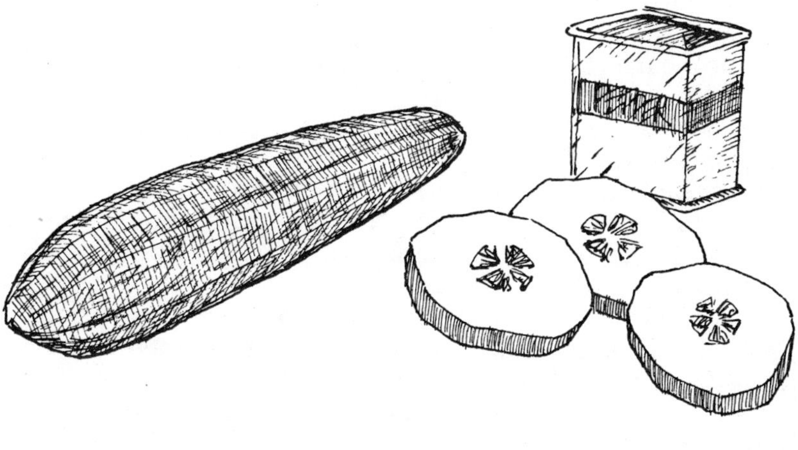

SAUERBRATEN WITH POTATO DUMPLINGS

The beef in this recipe is to be pickled for 3 to 5 days ahead (see step 2).

1 large onion, quartered and thinly sliced
3 teaspoons salt
2 bay leaves
1 teaspoon whole black peppercorns
2 cups vinegar
2 cups water
1 (4 to 5-pound) chuck, rump or round of beef
2 tablespoons butter
¼ cup brown sugar
¼ cup seedless raisins
4 to 6 ginger snaps, crumbled
1 cup sour cream (optional)
Potato Dumplings

1. Combine the onion, salt, bay leaves, peppercorns, vinegar and water in a large earthenware or glass container with a lid or cover.
2. Put the meat in the pickling solution in its container. Cover tightly and store in a cool place 3 to 5 days, turning meat twice daily.
3. Remove the meat from the pickling solution and pat dry. Strain the pickling solution, removing the peppercorns and bay leaves. Reserve the onion and pickling solution.
4. Melt the butter in a large kettle or Dutch oven. Add the reserved onion and cook, stirring, until translucent but not brown. Remove the onion and set aside.
5. Brown the meat on all sides in the kettle over moderate heat. Return the onion to the kettle. Add ½ cup pickling solution. Cover and simmer 2 hours or until the meat is almost tender. Add more pickling solution from time to time.
6. Remove the meat and set aside. Add the brown sugar and raisins to the liquid in the kettle. Add the ginger snap crumbs and cook, stirring, until smooth and thickened. Return the meat to the sauce and cook gently 1 hour.
7. Remove the meat from the sauce, slice and arrange on a warm platter. If desired, add sour cream to the sauce and heat through, but do not boil or the sauce will curdle.
8. Pour the sauce over the meat slices and serve immediately with **Potato Dumplings**.

Potato Dumplings

4 to 5 Idaho potatoes, well scrubbed
1½ cups flour
1 egg
1 tablespoon salt
Pinch of freshly ground white pepper
½ teaspoon grated onion
1 tablespoon fresh or dried marjoram
Small croutons
3 tablespoons butter
1 tablespoon fine bread crumbs

1. Place the unpeeled whole potatoes in a large pan. Cover with water. Bring to a boil, reduce heat and cook until tender. Drain, cool and chill thoroughly overnight.
2. Peel and finely grate the potatoes into a large bowl. Add 1 cup flour, the egg, salt, pepper, onion and marjoram and blend. Add another ½ cup flour to form a mixture that holds together.
3. Roll the mixture into balls about the size of an egg. Flatten and fill each with 3 to 4 croutons, reshaping into a ball.
4. Melt the butter and add the bread crumbs. Stir to blend. Set aside.
5. Cook the dumplings in boiling salted water 8 to 10 minutes or until done. Remove immediately and cover with the butter/crumb mixture. Serve with **Sauerbraten**.

Note: The Sauerbraten can be made early in the day. When reheating in the sauce, do not allow it to come to a boil or it will curdle. The Potato Dumplings can be formed ahead of time, covered and refrigerated. Do not cook them until serving time. They will reheat well.

APPLE SAUERKRAUT

4 strips bacon, diced
1 cup chopped onion
2 pounds sauerkraut
3 medium-size tart apples, peeled, cored and sliced
3 tablespoons brown sugar
1 tablespoon vinegar
1 teaspoon caraway seeds
Freshly ground black pepper
1 cup Beef Stock (see index) or ½ cup beef stock mixed with ½ cup white wine

1. Cook the bacon in a sauté pan until almost crisp. Remove and set aside.
2. Add the onion to the sauté pan and cook until translucent, not brown.
3. Add the sauerkraut, apples, brown sugar, vinegar, caraway seeds, pepper, bacon bits and meat stock (or combination of stock and wine).
4. Bring to a boil, reduce heat and simmer gently 20 minutes or until the apples slices are tender. Serve immediately.

Note: This dish can be made in advance and reheated.

APPLE CAKE

1½ teaspoons baking powder
½ teaspoon salt
2 tablespoons sugar
1 cup sifted flour
¼ cup butter
1 egg
½ cup milk
2½ cups peeled, thin-sliced apple
Topping Mixture

1. Add the baking powder, salt and sugar to the sifted flour. Sift again into a mixing bowl.
2. Preheat oven to 400°
3. Cut the butter into the dry ingredients to resemble fine meal.
4. Add the unbeaten egg and milk and beat until smooth and well blended. Spread into a well-greased 8" square baking pan.
5. Arrange the apple slices in rows over the batter. Sprinkle **Topping Mixture** over the apples and bake in preheated oven about 40 minutes or until the apples are tender.

Topping Mixture

¾ to 1 cup brown sugar
3 to 4 tablespoons butter, softened
½ teaspoon ground cinnamon
¼ teaspoon freshly grated nutmeg

Mix all ingredients together.

MARANGELLI'S

Marangelli's

Dinner for Four

Scampi Boccacio

Stracciatella Fiorentina
or
Pasta Novella with Zucchini and Fettuccini

Insalata in Bavaglia Gioconda

Breast of Chicken Caruso with Risotto Milanese

Asparagi Ravenna

Chocolate Tortoni

Wine:

With the Scampi–Ruffino Lugana, 1977
With the Chicken–Antinori Classico Riserva, 1975 or 1977

John Marangelli, Proprietor and Chef

MARANGELLI'S

John Marangelli, owner and chef of Marangelli's, is a wizard when it comes to Italian cuisine. He knows how to perfectly season a dish with fresh herbs, often the secret to really delicious cooking. Like any practicing chef, Marangelli likes to create new and exciting dishes.

His menu is extensive, but concentrates on the cuisine of central and northern Italy. The exclusive flavor of his cooking originated in the provinces of northern Italy, where generations of his family passed along time-honored village recipes, many of which are included on his extraordinary menu. Because of the unusual seasonings and manner of preparation, few Italian and Continental restaurants in America offer the exotic fare that Marangelli's does.

Born near Florence, Italy, Marangelli was inspired to go into professional cooking by his mother and a relative who had a small restaurant outside the city. He received his culinary education in Florence, and his cooking experience is vast. In addition to cooking in his home town, he served as chef in Naples and Paris before coming to America twenty-five years ago, originally to teach cooking. He was later hired by Milwaukee's Hotel Schroeder (now the Marc Plaza), where he was executive chef for eight years.

Marangelli thinks his restaurant is unique in that he does almost all the cooking on a personal basis for each patron—everything is cooked to order, with very little prepared in advance. "Scratch cooking is what I do here," he says. He relies on extra-fresh foods because he believes that they yield the best-tasting dishes. He has translated the nouvelle cuisine of France into what he calls *pasta novella*. "The concept of pasta novella is to capture the natural flavors and goodness of fresh vegetables while blending them in a sauce for pasta with a minimum of calories," he says.

8647 North Port Washington Road
Fox Point

SCAMPI BOCCACCIO

Crabmeat-Stuffed Scampi Wrapped in Veal

4 large (8 to 10-count) scampi, shells on
Crabmeat Filling *(see next page)*
4 (½-ounce) paper-thin slices veal, about 1" x 3"
3 bay leaves
1 large clove garlic, mashed
2 tablespoons chopped parsley
½ teaspoon fresh or dried mint
4 tablespoons butter
1 tablespoon good-quality olive oil
¼ cup dry white wine
1 tablespoon freshly grated Parmesan cheese
½ teaspoon dried oregano
Pinch of Colman's mustard
Pinch of salt
Pinch of freshly ground black pepper
1 lemon, cut into 4 wedges

1. Hold the scampi in one hand with soft-shell side up, head end nearest you and tail facing away. With scissors, cut the length of the scampi along one side where the hard and soft shells join. Push the soft shell to one side, taking care not to detach it from the hard shell. Slip a knife between the hard shell and the meat and loosen the meat from the shell. Do not completely remove the shell–leave it attached at the tail.
2. Preheat oven to 400°.
3. Devein each scampi and cut slightly into the flesh where the vein was, forming a cavity for stuffing. Do not cut completely through. Rinse and dry thoroughly.
4. Spread 1 teaspoon **Crabmeat Filling** the length of each scampi, in the slit. Wrap 1 slice veal around each to hold the stuffing in. Replace the stuffed meat back in the shell, securing each soft shell to its hard shell with a toothpick.

(continued next page)

5. Place the scampi side by side in a small ovenproof sauté pan with a bay leaf between each.
6. Mix the garlic with the parsley, mint, butter, oil, wine, Parmesan cheese, oregano, mustard, salt and pepper. Pour over the scampi in the pan and cover.
7. Bake in preheated oven 10 to 12 minutes.
8. Serve on warm plates, 1 scampi per plate. Divide the pan sauce over the scampi. Garnish each plate with a lemon wedge.

Note: The Scampi can be stuffed and refrigerated in advance. Bake just before serving, adding 5 minutes to the baking time if the scampi come cold from the refrigerator.

It is important not to destroy the shell when removing the scampi. The trick to this recipe is to cook the scampi without overcooking. Work with a hot oven and cook as directed, definitely not more than 20 minutes.

Be sure the scampi are very fresh. 'Scampi' does not refer to size, but rather to a European variety of shellfish. Scampi generally tend to be large, although there are some small ones.

"The feeling of my restaurant is the feeling I have for life, which is to devote my time to making people happy when they dine. I like to see people get excited about the food I cook. I'm happy creating dishes and discovering a person's food preferences so that I can create for him personally." Marangelli enjoys providing dinner in the European concept—as an evening's entertainment.

Crabmeat Filling

3 tablespoons butter
1 teaspoon finely chopped chives
1 tablespoon chopped mushrooms
1 small clove garlic, mashed
2 ounces frozen crab meat, thawed
1 teaspoon finely chopped parsley
1/8 cup cream sherry
1 tablespoon pineapple juice
3 tablespoons cream
1 small egg, lightly beaten
1 tablespoon freshly grated Parmesan cheese
Pinch of salt
Pinch of freshly ground white pepper

1. Melt the butter in a small saucepan over low heat. Add the chives and mushrooms and simmer 2 minutes; don't brown.
2. Add the garlic and crab meat to the pan, stirring. Simmer 1 minute; add the parsley.
3. Increase heat to medium-high and add the sherry, pineapple juice and cream. Reduce heat and simmer on low 1 to 2 minutes or until the liquid has almost evaporated.
4. Remove the pan from heat and whisk in the egg. Add the cheese, salt and pepper. Mix and allow to cool.

The hardest part of cooking in a restaurant, Marangelli believes, is timing. Having twenty orders at once taxes the chef. "Wouldn't it be nice if parties of two to four came in every fifteen minutes?" he asks.

STRACCIATELLA FIORENTINA
Rich Chicken Soup in the Florentine Style

1 quart **Rich Chicken Stock**
2 tablespoons diced celery
2 tablespoons diced carrot
2 tablespoons chopped onion
2 cups chopped fresh spinach, or 1 (10-ounce) package frozen chopped spinach, thawed and squeezed completely dry
⅓ cup diced tomato
2 eggs
2 tablespoons flour
3 tablespoons freshly grated Parmesan cheese
1 teaspoon melted butter
1 tablespoon chopped fresh parsley
Pinch of freshly grated nutmeg
Pinch of salt
Freshly grated Parmesan cheese for garnish (optional)

1. Place the stock in a soup pot, bring to simmer and cook 10 minutes. Add the celery, carrot, onion, spinach and tomato. Simmer 10 more minutes.
2. Whip the eggs in a small bowl with the flour, cheese, butter, parsley, nutmeg and salt to a smooth, batter-like consistency.
3. Bring the stock to a boil and gently pour in the batter, stirring constantly with the whisk, about 3 minutes. The batter mixture will be broken into flakes. Taste for seasoning and correct with salt and pepper if necessary.
4. Ladle into 4 soup bowls and top with a sprinkling of freshly grated Parmesan cheese, if desired. Serve immediately.

Note: This is an easy soup recipe that can be made in advance through step 2. The soup will reheat, but loses some of its fresh taste. Don't freeze.

The thing that makes this soup so delicious is a good homemade chicken stock made with lots of chicken bones. It gives the soup body and flavor. Be sure to whisk constantly when adding the batter or it will clump into a disagreeable mass. The spinach and tomato give the soup its Florentine character.

Rich Chicken Stock

Makes 5 cups.

2½ to 3 pounds chicken necks, backs and wings, rinsed in cold water
2 carrots, peeled and chunked
1 rib celery, chunked
1 medium-to-large ripe tomato
1 small onion, chunked
1½ teaspoons salt
4 to 5 sprigs parsley
1 small bay leaf
10 to 12 whole black peppercorns
1 small clove garlic
2 quarts cold water

1. Place the chicken necks, backs and wings in a large stock pot.
2. Add the carrots, celery, tomato, onion and salt to the stock pot.
3. Tie the parsley, bay leaf, peppercorns and garlic in cheesecloth. Add to the stock pot.
4. Add the water to the pot. Bring to a boil over high heat. Reduce heat and skim residue from the surface of the stock. Simmer slowly 2½ to 3 hours.
5. Remove from heat and cool at room temperature, uncovered. Taste for salt, adding more if necessary.
6. Strain to remove the chicken, vegetables and seasonings. Chill uncovered in refrigerator overnight. Remove congealed fat from the surface of the stock before using.

Extra stock can be frozen.

Marangelli urges the home cook to take cooking lessons from a professional chef if he has the opportunity. "Or at least learn the basic cooking techniques," he adds, adding that it's easy to do that now that cooking classes are popular and available in almost every city.

PASTA NOVELLA
with Zucchini and Fettuccini

1 quart lightly salted water
1 pound zucchini,
thinly sliced on the diagonal
Salt
2 tablespoons vegetable oil
3 tablespoons butter
1 large clove garlic, mashed to paste consistency
1 clove garlic, slightly crushed
1 tablespoon chopped parsley
¼ teaspoon chopped fresh mint
Juice of ¼ lemon
5 ounces dry fettuccini, cooked in lightly salted water, drained, and kept hot

1. Put enough water to barely cover the zucchini in a pot and salt lightly. Bring to a boil and add the zucchini, cooking 2 to 3 minutes. Drain the water, leaving 3 to 4 tablespoons in the pot. Taste the zucchini and add salt if necessary.
2. Add 1 tablespoon oil, the butter and mashed garlic; toss to combine.
3. Rub a large bowl with the slightly crushed garlic; discard garlic. Add the remaining tablespoon of oil to the bowl, then the parsley, mint, lemon juice and hot cooked drained pasta.

The trick to this dish is to cook the zucchini so it still has some crunch. The blending of salt and lemon juice is crucial; balance is important so that the taste is neither too salty nor too sour.

Omit the mint if fresh mint isn't available.

This is a Marangelli specialty, capitalizing on pasta novella or cooking a sauce for a light pasta dish that is relatively low in calories.

INSALATA IN BAVAGLIA GIOCONDA

Salad of Vegetables in Gorgonzola Dressing

1 small head Bibb lettuce
1 fresh artichoke bottom
¼ cup lemon juice
⅓ cucumber (approximately)
½ cup seeded sliced tomato or cherry tomatoes
½ cup very thinly sliced fresh fennel stalk, with some leaves
½ cup thinly sliced fresh mushrooms
Gorgonzola Dressing *(see next page)*
1 hard-cooked egg, chopped
Freshly ground black pepper

1. Separate, wash and dry the lettuce leaves. Select 4 large leaves; reserve the remainder for other use.
2. Blanch the artichoke bottom in boiling salted water 30 seconds. Place in the lemon juice to prevent discoloration. Slice.
3. Seed and partially peel the cucumber. Slice thinly on the diagonal to produce approximately ½ cup.
4. Combine the artichoke, cucumber slices, tomato, fennel and mushrooms with **Gorgonzola Dressing.**
5. Make a cup of each lettuce leaf and place on individual chilled salad plates. Divide the vegetable mixture among the lettuce cups, molding into rounded shapes. Sprinkle with chopped egg and pepper.

If you can't find fresh fennel, use celery instead.

Gorgonzola Dressing

1 clove garlic, mashed to paste
8 flat anchovy filets
1 tablespoon red wine vinegar
3 tablespoons freshly squeezed lemon juice
¼ cup good-quality olive oil
½ teaspoon dried oregano
2 ounces crumbled Gorgonzola cheese

1. Put the mashed garlic and anchovies on a cutting board and chop together. Transfer to a small mixing bowl.
2. Whip in the vinegar and lemon juice with a whisk.
3. Add the remaining ingredients and whip lightly with the whisk to combine.

Note: Be sure when making the dressing to keep the cheese in crumbs. Don't whip to a smooth consistency. The dressing can be made ahead, but the rest of the preparation should be done no more than 1 hour before serving.

It is important to select the freshest, best-quality vegetables and to cut them very thinly. The dressing is simple to make, but it is essential to use a good-quality olive oil like Bertolli or Berio. If you can't afford the best olive oil, don't settle for a cheap brand. Substitute vegetable oil instead.

BREAST OF CHICKEN CARUSO
with Risotto Milanese

2 slices bacon or salt pork, diced small
½ cup olive oil or vegetable oil
¼ pound very fresh chicken livers
Flour
2 whole chicken breasts, boned
¾ cup finely chopped onion
2 tablespoons chopped chives or green onions
2 tablespoons chopped green pepper
2 bay leaves
1 cup quartered fresh mushrooms
2 tablespoons butter
7 ounces dry red wine
1 ounce Marsala or sweet vermouth
1½ teaspoons tomato paste
1 tablespoon dried rosemary
1½ teaspoons sage
Salt and freshly ground black pepper to taste
Chicken Stock (optional-see index)
Risotto Milanese *(see next page)*
Tomato strips or pimiento strips for garnish

1. Render the fat from the bacon or salt pork in a heavy skillet over medium heat. Increase heat, add the oil and heat until hot. Add the chicken livers, stirring, and sauté 1 minute. Remove from the skillet with a slotted spoon and set aside.
2. Lower heat. Lightly flour the chicken breasts and place in the skillet, skin side down. Lightly brown on both sides, 4 to 5 minutes.
3. Add the onion, chives and green pepper and simmer 8 to 10 minutes. Add the bay leaves and mushrooms.
4. Increase heat to high and add the butter. Bring to a sizzle. Add the livers, both wines, tomato paste, rosemary, sage, salt and pepper. Stir to combine the ingredients, adding some hot water or Chicken Stock to thin the sauce if necessary.
5. Cover the pan, lower heat and cook 30 to 35 minutes.
6. Remove the chicken breasts and cut each in half lengthwise. Place on one side of a warm platter, topping with the chicken livers. Place **Risotto Milanese** on the opposite side of the platter.

(continued next page)

7. Taste the sauce in the pan and add more salt and pepper if necessary. Pour the sauce over the chicken breasts. Garnish with tomato or pimiento strips and serve immediately.

The regulation of the heat is essential with the sauce for the chicken. The sauce shouldn't be too thin or too thick. Also be careful when adding salt to the chicken because the bacon or salt pork will have some salt. Another secret is to just slightly cook the livers so they won't break up when you are making the sauce.

Risotto Milanese

3½ cups Chicken Stock (see index)
3 tablespoons butter
¼ cup finely chopped onion
⅛ cup veal or beef marrow
1 cup long-grain rice
1/16 teaspoon powdered saffron
2 tablespoons butter, softened
¼ cup freshly grated Parmesan cheese

1. Put the stock in a saucepan and bring to a simmer over low heat.
2. Preheat oven to 350°.
3. Melt 3 tablespoons butter in a heavy 2-quart pot with a tight-fitting lid. Cook the onion in the butter over moderate heat, 7 to 8 minutes or until soft but not brown.
4. Stir in the marrow. Add the rice and stir 4 to 5 minutes until all the rice is covered with butter.
5. Place the saffron in the simmering stock to dissolve. Pour the stock over the rice, stir well, cover the pot and bake in preheated oven 25 to 30 minutes or until all the stock is absorbed.
6. Transfer the rice to a shallow pan and gently stir in the softened butter and grated cheese with 2 forks. Serve at once.

Note: The chicken can be made early in the day along with the sauce. Reheat the chicken breasts and livers in a 300° oven, and reheat the sauce separately in a saucepan. The risotto can be made ahead and reheated in a 300° oven 10 minutes. When making the risotto, be sure to put it in a heavy pot with a tight-fitting lid and have the oven preheated.

If marrow is unavailable, substitute 2 tablespoons butter.

ASPARAGI RAVENNA

1¼ cups unsalted Chicken Stock (see index), or water
¼ cup finely chopped celery
¼ cup finely chopped cauliflower
1 pound asparagus
¾ cup seasoned Chicken Stock (see index)
¼ cup chopped tomato
1 egg at room temperature, beaten
2 tablespoons freshly grated Parmesan cheese
4 tablespoons butter

1. Put the unsalted Chicken Stock or water in a saucepan and bring to simmer. Add the celery and cauliflower.
2. Wash the asparagus, breaking off tough ends. Place in a small rectangular pan and add the seasoned Chicken Stock. Simmer 3 to 4 minutes on the stove top. Remove from heat and allow the asparagus to set in the stock 2 to 3 minutes.
3. Pour the juice off the asparagus and add juice to the vegetables in the saucepan. Keep the asparagus warm.
4. Reduce the liquid in the saucepan over medium-high heat to 1 cup. Add the tomato and continue to reduce the stock to ½ cup.
5. Preheat oven to 400°.
6. Vigorously beat the egg, adding a few drops of warm water.
7. Take the vegetable pan off the heat and pour the beaten egg little by little into the reduced stock, stirring continuously with a whisk.
8. Return the saucepan to very low heat and stir continuously with the whisk until the stock develops the consistency of Hollandaise sauce.
9. Stir in the cheese and butter and pour over the hot asparagus. Place in preheated oven 2 to 3 minutes. Serve immediately.

Note: The critical part of this recipe is to add the egg very gradually to the reduced stock. If the egg is added too fast, the sauce will break. This sauce is thickened with only the single egg rather than flour, cornstarch or arrowroot.

The sauce can be made ahead, if desired.

CHOCOLATE TORTONI

¼ pound semisweet chocolate, coarsely chopped
¼ cup light rum
2 tablespoons cherry brandy
2 tablespoons white crème de cacao
4 tablespoons butter
1 cup powdered sugar (approximately)
2 eggs, separated
⅓ cup slivered blanched almonds, toasted
1½ cups whipping cream
½ teaspoon vanilla
Few drops of lemon extract
3 to 4 drops anise oil
1 teaspoon almond extract
Pinch of salt

1. Put the chocolate in the top of a double boiler over hot water. Melt and stir in the rum, cherry brandy and crème de cacao. Remove from heat and let cool to room temperature.
2. Cream the butter and 2 tablespoons powdered sugar, adding the egg yolks one at a time. Stir in the cooled chocolate mixture. Stir in the almonds and chill in refrigerator.
3. Whip 1 cup cream to stiff peaks with ¾ cup powdered sugar, vanilla, lemon extract, anise oil and almond extract. Fold into the chocolate mixture; set aside.
4. Beat the egg whites with a pinch of salt to soft peaks. Gently fold in the chocolate mixture. Spoon into 4 individual metal molds or one miniature loaf pan. Be sure to rinse the molds in cold water for easier unmolding. Freeze.
5. Whip the remaining ½ cup cream with powdered sugar to taste. Unmold the individual molds and garnish with whipped cream. Or, unmold the loaf pan, cut dessert into 4 slices and garnish each with whipped cream.

During his career Marangelli has prepared meals for movie stars, statesmen and other celebrities. "I was requested to cook a dinner for President and Mrs. Kennedy when they were in Milwaukee. She so liked the dessert that she took some of it to the White House with her," he adds.

京園酒家

PEKING GARDEN EAST

Dinner for Four

Mandarin Egg Roll

Hot and Sour Soup

Beef with Chinese Black Mushrooms

Chicken with Peanuts and Red Pepper

Crabmeat with Straw Mushrooms

Mixed Chinese Greens

Paper-Thin Chinese Rosettes

Wine:

Tai-Shan

Ada and Paul Lie, Proprietors
Sam Lee, Chef

PEKING GARDEN EAST

The Peking Garden East is a popular restaurant in Milwaukee with an interesting history. It got its start in the early seventies in Madison, Wisconsin, when Ada and Paul Lie opened a restaurant offering all of the regional styles of Chinese cooking, from Cantonese to Szechuan. At the time, Mrs. Lie was working on her doctorate in psychology at the University of Wisconsin. Her husband drove her to classes in Madison each night from their home in Milwaukee, ninety miles away. They decided to open the restaurant to give Mr. Lie something to do while his wife attended classes.

The restaurant was relocated in Milwaukee in 1973, with another branch in nearby Grafton in 1977. Both restaurants recently closed for a short while, reopening in March—much to the delight of Peking Garden and regional Chinese cooking fans.

Cantonese, Hunan-Szechuan, Mandarin and Shanghai styles of cuisine are featured at the restaurant. Also offered are Mongolian hot pot dinners and dim sum. Dim sum describes the service of a variety of appetizer-like items which are presented at tableside and selected by the diner. In all, more than 150 different items are offered on the menu.

At the Peking Garden East, Paul Lie works with Chef Sam Lee to develop such innovations as a low-fat, salt-free approach to Chinese cooking, which is now available upon request. Chef Lee was trained in China and exemplifies Mrs. Lie's conception of the good chef: "He must have a lot of experience, and has to want to work hard," she says, and adds that "he doesn't mind taking the time to prepare food from scratch." The secret to Chinese cooking, Mrs. Lie observes, lies in early planning and organization. All foods must be prepared in advance because the cooking is done very quickly in a wok.

According to Mrs. Lie, the Peking Garden East was the first restaurant in Wisconsin to offer Mandarin and Szechuan cooking. The Lies, who claim no single preference among the varied styles of Chinese cuisine, found themselves in the position of educating their public. But people learned quickly and willingly about the regional dishes—because they taste good.

12741 North Port Washington Road
Mequon

MANDARIN EGG ROLL

1½ cups dried black mushrooms (approximately)
5¼ cups vegetable oil
½ teaspoon crushed fresh garlic
½ teaspoon crushed fresh ginger root
½ cup cooked ground pork
1 tablespoon cooking wine
½ cup cooked shrimp
1 cup shredded bamboo shoots
1 cup bean sprouts
1 cup shredded celery
1 scallion, shredded
1 teaspoon sesame seed oil
Salt and freshly ground white pepper to taste
8 rice-flour egg roll wrappers
1 egg white, lightly beaten

1. Soak the mushrooms in hot water 15 minutes. Drain, cut off tough stems and shred to make ½ cup.
2. Place ¼ cup oil in a wok over high heat until hot. Add the garlic, ginger and pork. Stir-fry 2 minutes.
3. Add the cooking wine and shrimp and stir-fry 2 minutes. Add the mushrooms and remaining vegetables and stir-fry 2 minutes.
4. Add the sesame seed oil and salt and pepper to taste. Mix. Drain off excess liquid and set the vegetable mixture aside.
5. In a clean wok, heat 5 cups vegetable oil to the boiling point, about 400°.
6. Working with one at a time, lay the egg roll wrappers on the counter and place one-eighth of the reserved vegetable mixture on one end of each. Moisten the edges of the wrapper with the egg white and roll the wrapper, tucking in the ends at both sides of wrapper as you roll. (Egg white acts as a sealer for the wrapper.)
7. Deep-fry the egg roll about 5 to 10 minutes. Remove from the oil and drain on paper towels. Continue to roll and cook egg rolls one at a time. Serve with sweet and sour sauce, allowing 2 egg rolls per person.

Note: The filling can be made well in advance. Deep-fried egg rolls can be frozen. To serve, thaw and reheat in deep-fryer just to heat through. Do not reheat so long as to cook the egg roll further.

Egg-roll wrappers will dry out quickly, so it is important to roll and cook them one by one. Be sure not to brown them too much and don't let them sit too long before serving or they will become soggy.

HOT AND SOUR SOUP

6 to 8 cloud ear mushrooms
6 to 8 tiger lily buds
1 quart Chicken Stock (see index)
1 teaspoon salt
1 tablespoon soy sauce
½ cup bamboo shoots, drained, rinsed in cold water and shredded
¼ pound boneless pork, trimmed of all fat, sliced 1½″ x 2″
2 squares (3″ by 3″ by 1½″ each) fresh Chinese bean curd, drained, rinsed in cold water and shredded
¼ teaspoon ground white pepper
2 tablespoons white vinegar
2 tablespoons cornstarch, mixed with 3 tablespoons cold water
1 egg, lightly beaten
2 tablespoons sesame oil
1 scallion, finely chopped, including green part

1. Soak the cloud ear mushrooms and tiger lily buds in ½ cup warm water for 10 minutes. Drain and shred the mushrooms. Cut the tiger lily buds in 1″ lengths.
2. Have the remaining ingredients measured and placed nearby for cooking.
3. Place the stock, salt, soy sauce, bamboo shoots, pork, mushrooms and tiger lily buds in a 3-quart saucepan.
4. Bring to a boil over high heat. Immediately reduce heat to low, cover the pan and simmer 3 minutes.
5. Add the bean curd, pepper and vinegar. Return to a boil. Stir the cornstarch mixture to recombine it and pour into the saucepan. Stir until the soup thickens.
6. Slowly pour in the beaten egg, stirring gently.
7. Remove from heat and pour into a serving bowl. Stir in the sesame seed oil and sprinkle the chopped scallion on top of the soup. Serve immediately.

Note: The soup can be made in advance to the point of adding the cornstarch.

Do not omit the vinegar or ground white pepper because they work together to give the soup a hot and sour taste.

BEEF WITH CHINESE BLACK MUSHROOMS

10 Chinese black mushrooms
½ pound flank steak
4 teaspoons cornstarch
1 egg white, lightly beaten
½ cup plus 2 tablespoons vegetable oil
1 teaspoon crushed fresh ginger root
1 teaspoon crushed fresh garlic
1 cup bamboo shoots, drained, rinsed in cold water and cubed
1 teaspoon cooking wine
1 teaspoon dark soy sauce
½ cup Chicken Stock (see index)
Salt and pepper to taste
1 scallion, shredded

1. Place the mushrooms in a bowl, cover with 1 cup warm water and soak 10 minutes. Drain, discard tough stems and quarter the caps. Set aside.
2. Trim all fat from the meat and slice in thin strips across the grain of the meat. Place in a bowl. Mix 2 teaspoons cornstarch with 4 teaspoons cold water; add to the meat. Add the egg white and stir to coat meat. Set aside. Mix the remaining 2 teaspoons cornstarch with 4 teaspoons cold water; reserve.
3. Heat a wok over high heat 30 seconds. Add ½ cup oil and swirl it around in the wok. Add ½ teaspoon ginger, ½ teaspoon garlic and the beef mixture and stir-fry 2 to 3 minutes. Remove from the wok, draining excess oil.
4. Put 2 tablespoons oil in a clean wok and heat until hot. Stir-fry the remaining ½ teaspoon ginger and ½ teaspoon garlic until brown. Add the reserved beef mixture, bamboo shoots, reserved black mushrooms and cooking wine. Stir-fry over high heat 1 minute.
5. Add the soy sauces, Chicken Stock and salt and pepper to taste. Thicken with the reserved cornstarch mixture, stirring gently. Pour into a serving dish and garnish with the shredded scallion.

Be sure not to overcook the beef or it will become tough. You will have to work quickly.

CHICKEN WITH PEANUTS AND RED PEPPER

½ pound boneless chicken breast, skinned and cubed
Salt
1 egg white, lightly beaten
3½ teaspoons cornstarch
½ cup vegetable oil
½ teaspoon crushed fresh ginger root
½ teaspoon crushed fresh garlic
6 pieces dried red pepper
3 scallions, chopped
½ teaspoon sugar
2 tablespoons dark soy sauce
1 tablespoon cooking sherry
1 teaspoon vinegar
Ground black pepper to taste
½ cup peanuts

1. Place the chicken meat, ½ teaspoon salt, egg white and ½ teaspoon cornstarch in a bowl and mix. Set aside. Mix the remaining 3 teaspoons cornstarch with 2 tablespoons cold water and reserve.
2. Put 6 tablespoons oil in a wok and heat to warm. Drain the chicken and add to the oil, cooking just until done over low heat. Remove and set aside.
3. Heat 2 tablespoons oil in a clean wok and add the ginger, garlic and red pepper and stir-fry 30 seconds.
4. Add the reserved chicken, scallions, sugar, soy sauce, sherry and vinegar and stir-fry 1 minute. Add salt and pepper to taste.
5. Stir in the reserved cornstarch mixture until thickened. Add the peanuts and mix to coat.

Take care not to overcook the chicken. This is a hot dish. Be sure not to cook the red pepper too long. You can reduce the amount of red pepper if you don't like hot Szechuan dishes.

CRABMEAT WITH STRAW MUSHROOMS

3 tablespoons vegetable oil
2 small cloves garlic, chopped
¼ pound frozen Alaska king crab, thawed and drained
2 teaspoons white wine
8 ounces canned straw mushrooms, drained
8 ounces canned baby corn, drained
2 ounces fresh snow pea pods, tips trimmed
1 teaspoon salt
¼ teaspoon ground white pepper
1 cup water
1 teaspoon cornstarch, mixed with 2 teaspoons cold water
2 teaspoons sesame seed oil

1. Bring the oil to high heat in a wok. Add the garlic, crab, wine, mushrooms, corn and pea pods. Stir-fry 2 minutes.
2. Add the salt, white pepper and water, then add the cornstarch mixture and stir-fry until thickened.
3. Remove from heat. Add the sesame seed oil and stir to combine.

Note: This dish should be cooked at the last minute to ensure maximum freshness. It must be served hot.

MIXED CHINESE GREENS

8 dried black mushrooms
2 teaspoons vegetable oil
½ teaspoon crushed fresh ginger root
½ teaspoon crushed fresh garlic
1 cup sliced broccoli
1 cup sliced celery
½ cup sliced bamboo shoots
½ cup button mushrooms
1 green pepper, sliced in thin strips
1 tomato, quartered and seeded
½ cup straw mushrooms
1 cup Chinese celery cabbage (bok choy), sliced
2 tablespoons cooking wine
½ cup Chicken Stock (see index)
1 tablespoon cornstarch, mixed with 2 tablespoons cold water
1 teaspoon light soy sauce
Salt and pepper to taste
1 teaspoon sesame seed oil

1. Soak the black mushrooms in hot water 10 minutes. Drain and remove tough stems.
2. Heat the oil in a wok over high heat.
3. When it is medium-hot, add the ginger and garlic and stir-fry a few seconds. Add the broccoli, celery, bamboo shoots, black mushrooms, button mushrooms, green pepper, tomato, straw mushrooms and celery cabbage. Stir-fry 3 minutes.
4. Add the wine and Chicken Stock. Stir in the cornstarch mixture until thickened.
5. Add the soy sauce, salt, pepper, and sesame seed oil. Stir to mix and serve immediately.

Don't overcook the vegetables. They should be crisp, yet cooked.

PAPER-THIN CHINESE ROSETTES

1 cup sifted flour
1 cup milk
1 egg
1 tablespoon sugar
½ teaspoon salt
2 tablespoons sesame seeds
5 cups vegetable oil

1. Stir together the flour, milk, egg, sugar, salt and sesame seeds until smooth.
2. Put the oil in a wok and heat to 365°. Dip a rosette iron with a mold attached into the hot oil and shake off excess oil.
3. Dip the hot oiled rosette mold into the batter, shaking off excess batter. Hold in the hot oil. When slightly brown, nudge the rosette off the mold using the tip of a knife. Let the rosette fall back into the hot oil.
4. Repeat the process until all the batter is used.
5. When the rosettes are brown on one side, turn over and brown on the other side. Remove from the oil and drain on paper towels.

Note: These can be made in advance. If they get soggy, reheat in a 300° oven until crispy.

Don't leave the rosettes in the oil too long. They should be lightly browned.

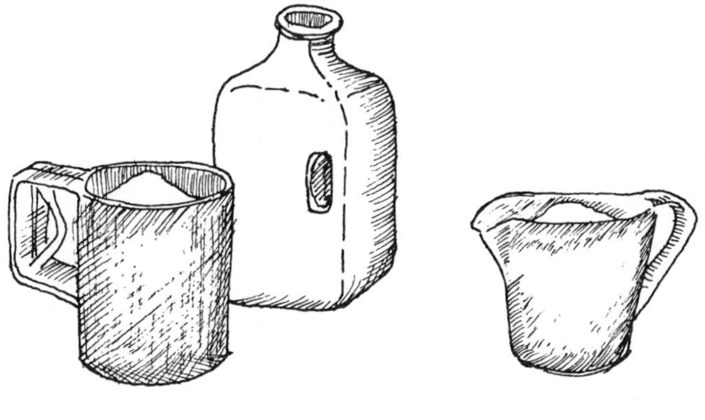

the POSTILION

Dinner for Six

Bay Scallops Sautéed in Butter and Caper Sauce

Essence of Cucumber Soup

Boston Lettuce in Walnut Oil and Champagne Vinaigrette

Chicken in Lemon Sauce

Steamed Cauliflower with Buttered Nutmeg Sauce

Potato Rissolée

Crème Caramel

Wine:

With the Scallops—Blanc Fuissé
With the Chicken—Bernkasteler Doktor Mosel, 1979

Mme. Liane Kuony, Chef and Proprietor

POSTILION GREAT HOUSE

The Postilion Great House restaurant occupies half of the main floor of the Matthew Keenan townhouse, an 1860s Italian-Victorian mansion on the East Side that has become a Milwaukee landmark.

Madame Liane Kuony, Wisconsin's doyenne of French cuisine, is proprietor and principal chef at the two-year-old restaurant. It is an extension of the Postilion Restaurant, which she opened thirty years ago in conjunction with a cooking school in her farm home outside Fond du Lac. Though the Fond du Lac restaurant has closed, the cooking school still operates, and a Postilion II School of Culinary Art and gift shop occupy the other half of the Milwaukee establishment.

Those who dine at the Postilion Great House—a salon restaurant—are greeted at the door by Mme. Kuony, who usually is wearing one of the hats which are her hallmark. She directs guests to the high-ceilinged dining room where no more than thirty-two can be seated at one time. The atmosphere is one of serenity as fresh flowers, candles, china, linen, engraved silver flatware and soft music set the mood. The mood is much like that of a dinner party in a private home.

There are no printed menus; the courses of the fixed-price menu change daily and according to the season. Mme. Kuony details the evening's bill of fare to each table, explaining the foods if necessary. "Madame," as she is frequently called, is responsible for selecting each day's menu. She also oversees its preparation in the kitchen, where cooking students refine their skills. Fresh foods, individually prepared, are the trademark at this very private restaurant. Smoking is not allowed, except with dessert and coffee. As may be imagined, reservations are a must.

775 North Jefferson Street

BAY SCALLOPS
Sautéed in Butter and Caper Sauce

3 cups Boston bay scallops, patted dry
Salt
Freshly ground white pepper
Flour
6 tablespoons butter
1 tablespoon capers, undrained
2 tablespoons chopped fresh parsley
Juice of 1 lemon

1. Lightly salt and pepper the scallops and dredge in flour, shaking off the excess flour.
2. Melt the butter in a large skillet over medium heat, but do not let brown. Add the scallops, increase heat to high and sauté, stirring constantly, until the scallops are opaque—3 to 5 minutes.
3. Add the capers and their juice, parsley and lemon juice. Mix well and serve immediately.

ESSENCE OF CUCUMBER SOUP

7 cups Chicken Stock (see index)
5 large cucumbers, peeled and quartered
1 large cucumber, peeled and diced
3 egg yolks, beaten
1 cup heavy cream
1 teaspoon chopped fresh dill
Salt and pepper to taste

1. Place 1½ quarts Chicken Stock and the quartered cucumbers in a saucepan and simmer on low heat 1 hour. Strain, reserving the liquid. Discard the cucumber chunks or reserve for other use.
2. Place the diced cucumber in a small saucepan and add remaining Chicken Stock just to cover. Cook on medium heat until the cucumber is barely tender. Set aside.
3. Blend the egg yolks with half the cream and add to the reserved cucumber stock, mixing well. Add the rest of the cream, the dill, and salt and pepper to taste.
4. Bring the soup just to the boiling point. Remove from heat and divide among 6 soup bowls, garnishing each with the reserved poached cucumber.

The secret in this recipe is to use a robust Chicken Stock. The best cucumbers for this soup are pickling cucumbers. The cucumber chunks from the stock may be used in tomato or other vegetable soups.

BOSTON LETTUCE
in Walnut Oil and Champagne Vinaigrette

1 teaspoon sea salt
12 whole black peppercorns
¼ cup walnut oil
¼ cup champagne vinegar
3 small heads Boston lettuce, washed, drained and crisped

1. Place the sea salt and peppercorns in a mortar and thoroughly crush with a pestle. Place in a small mixing bowl.
2. Very gradually add the oil, stirring constantly. Add the vinegar gradually, also stirring constantly.
3. Pour over the prepared lettuce, divide among 6 salad plates and serve immediately.

CHICKEN IN LEMON SAUCE

2 (3 to 3½-pound) roasting chickens, trussed
Zest of 2 lemons
Salt
Freshly ground black pepper
6 tablespoons butter, melted
½ clove garlic, finely chopped
½ cup Chicken Stock (see index)
Juice of ½ lemon
¼ cup butter, room temperature

1. Preheat oven to 375°.
2. Place the trussed roasting chickens on a cutting board and rub the outsides with the zest of 1 lemon, taking care to remove all the zest after rubbing. Season the outsides with salt and freshly ground black pepper. Place the chickens in an open roasting pan and roast 1¾ hours in preheated oven, basting occasionally with the melted butter.
3. When the chickens are done, remove from the pan and place on a serving platter. Remove the trussing strings and disjoint the chickens.
4. Slice the remaining lemon zest into juliennes. Blanch briefly in boiling water and drain. Add the blanched zest, garlic, Chicken Stock and lemon juice to the drippings in the pan. Bring to a boil, scraping the bottom of the pan with a wooden spoon to remove the browned bits of chicken. Add the room temperature butter and stir to melt. Pour some of the sauce over the chicken and pass the remainder at the table.

It is important to use only the lemon zest—the yellow part of the peel—as the white membrane will make the dish bitter.

STEAMED CAULIFLOWER
with Buttered Nutmeg Sauce

1 medium-size head cauliflower
4 tablespoons butter
Whole nutmeg

1. Core the cauliflower, retaining as many green leaves as possible. Place in a kettle large enough to hold it. Add enough salted water for steaming; steam until tender when pierced with a knife. Remove the cauliflower and place on a serving platter.
2. Melt the butter in a small skillet and cook over medium heat until browned, about 5 minutes. Pour over the cauliflower and grate nutmeg over. Serve immediately.

It is important to select a young cauliflower, not one that is old and tough.

POTATO RISSOLEE

18 very small new potatoes
¼ pound butter
Freshly chopped parsley for garnish

1. Preheat oven to 375°.
2. Place the potatoes in a pan with enough salted water to cover and cook over medium heat until just tender. Drain off the water and peel the potatoes.
3. Melt the butter in a large skillet that can be put in the oven. Add the potatoes and sauté just to completely cover the potatoes with butter.
4. Place the skillet in preheated oven and bake 20 to 25 minutes, stirring the potatoes occasionally so they brown evenly.
5. Remove from the oven and place in a serving bowl. Garnish with parsley and serve immediately.

CREME CARAMEL

1 cup sugar
4 egg yolks, beaten
1 pint heavy cream, heated to lukewarm
Inside pulp of 1/4 vanilla bean, mixed with 3/4 cup extra-fine sugar
Good pinch of salt

1. Preheat oven to 325°.
2. Place the sugar in a skillet and slowly melt over medium heat, stirring occasionally, until liquefied. Pour into 6 (6-ounce) custard cups, tilting the cups so that the caramelized sugar coats the bottom of each cup. Reserve.
3. Mix the egg yolks, cream, vanilla/sugar mixture and salt. Pour into the prepared cups and place the cups in a large shallow pan. Fill the pan with hot water so that it comes three-fourths up the outsides of the cups. Bake 22 to 26 minutes in preheated oven. The dessert is done when the surface is glossy and a toothpick inserted in the center comes out clean.
4. Refrigerate to chill thoroughly before serving.

It is best to coat the custard cups with the caramelized sugar the day before preparing the dessert. The longer the finished caramel is allowed to rest, the more the caramel on the bottom of the cups will become like a sauce.

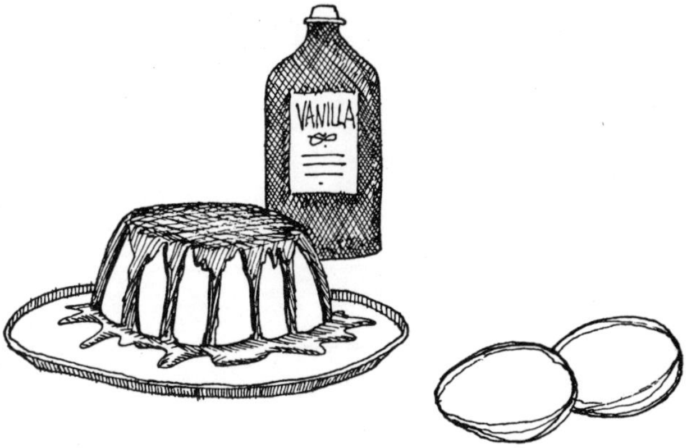

The Proud Popover

Dinner for Six

Popovers

Indian Corn Chowder Garnished with Bacon

Fresh Spinach Salad with Sweet-Sour Dressing

Chicken Alouette with Wine Sauce

Ratatouille

Cream Puffs with Strawberries and Raspberry Cassis Sauce

Wine:

California Chablis

Ronald P. Siepmann, Proprietor
James Rafenstein, Chef

THE PROUD POPOVER

The Proud Popover is a unique restaurant in Stonewood Village in Brookfield where colonial charm and atmosphere greet each diner. The restaurant furnishings complement the colonial theme with antiques dating from the Civil War. Founded in 1975, the Proud Popover was the idea of entrepreneur Ronald P. Siepmann and chef James Rafenstein. Friendly service and homemade foods, featuring fantastically large and flavorful popovers, are the twin cornerstones of this restaurant.

The concept of the Proud Popover was so popular that a major national food company franchised the restaurant, temporarily controlling the Brookfield restaurant as well. Ownership of the original Proud Popover has now returned to its creators.

Popovers, baked fresh each day, accompany every dinner. They also star as the entrée in several selections, including popovers filled with shrimp and chicken, tender beef and mushrooms in gravy, or creamed chicken with fresh mushrooms delicately flavored with sherry. The food is freshly made from scratch, and the chef enjoys preparing dishes not listed on the menu.

Chef Rafenstein entered the restaurant business as a dishwasher at the age of fifteen. By the time he was eighteen, he was managing a restaurant and its kitchen in Milwaukee. Rafenstein believes that a chef must develop a good palate if he is to be successful in his labors, and that organization is the key to successful cooking and entertaining at home as well as on the job.

17700 West Capitol Drive
Brookfield

POPOVERS

2½ cups milk
5 large eggs
½ teaspoon kosher salt
2½ cups flour

1. Preheat oven to 400°.
2. Combine the milk, eggs and salt in a bowl and whip by hand with a wire whisk.
3. Slowly add the flour, stirring until the batter is the consistency of pancake batter.
4. Spray a 12-muffin pan with low-water-content oil. Fill the tins to the top with the batter.
5. Bake 30 minutes in preheated oven. Reduce oven heat if the popovers begin to brown before the bottoms are firm.

Serve hot Popovers with sweet butter and clover honey.

A gas oven is best for making popovers. If you don't have one, be sure to preheat your electric oven. Use an oven thermometer to check that your oven heats to the specified temperature. It's important to mix the batter for the popovers by hand, taking care not to overbeat.

INDIAN CORN CHOWDER
Garnished with Bacon

1 quart water
7 chicken bouillon cubes
½ teaspoon ground white pepper
½ cup chopped onion
1 cup sliced mushrooms
2 cups frozen corn
1 cup diced potatoes
¼ pound butter
½ cup flour
2 cups milk
Cooked bacon bits for garnish

1. Place the water, bouillon cubes, pepper, onion, mushrooms, corn and potatoes in a kettle. Bring to a simmer over medium heat; allow to simmer 15 minutes. Drain off the broth and reserve; set the vegetables aside.
2. Melt the butter in the kettle. When bubbling, add the flour, stirring vigorously with a wire whisk. Add the reserved hot broth slowly, stirring constantly, until the mixture is smooth.
3. Slowly add the milk, stirring. Add the reserved vegetables. Heat to serving temperature. Add hot water to thin to desired consistency if needed.
4. Serve hot in 6 soup bowls, garnishing each with bacon bits.

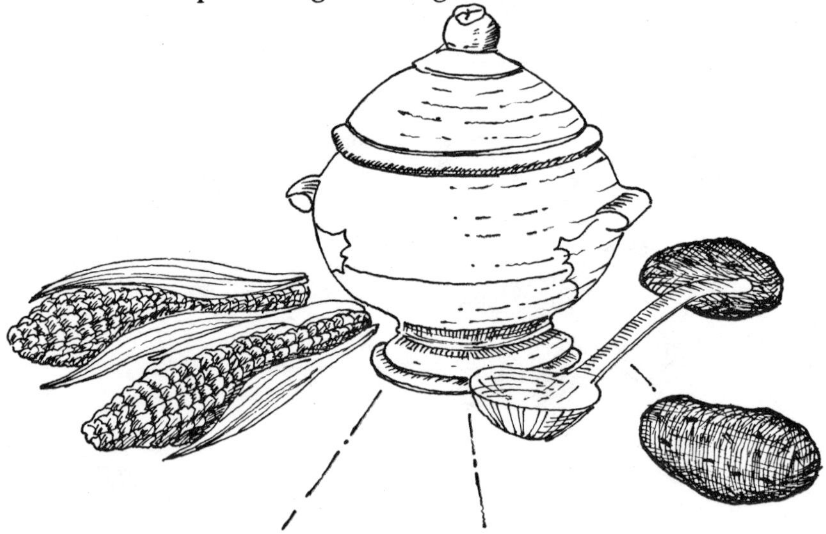

FRESH SPINACH SALAD
with Sweet-Sour Dressing

1 pound fresh spinach
1 cup sliced mushrooms
½ cup crisp bacon bits
2 hard-cooked eggs, sliced
Sweet-Sour Dressing

1. Wash the spinach well and remove stems. Tear into 2" pieces and crisp in refrigerator.
2. Put the spinach in a salad bowl and add the mushrooms, bacon bits and egg slices. Add the dressing and toss gently. Serve, dividing among 6 salad plates.

Sweet-Sour Dressing

1½ tablespoons fresh lemon juice
¼ cup tarragon vinegar
1½ tablespoons Grey Poupon mustard
2 tablespoons sugar
½ teaspoon salt
½ teaspoon freshly ground black pepper
1½ teaspoons tarragon leaves
1 cup olive oil

1. Place all ingredients except the oil in a mixer bowl and beat well.
2. At low speed, slowly add the oil until the dressing thickens. Put in a jar and shake before using.

Be sure to clean the spinach well to remove any sand. If the dressing is refrigerated, it will thicken slightly. Let it return to room temperature and shake well before using.

CHICKEN ALOUETTE
with Wine Sauce

6 (8-ounce) chicken breasts, skinned, boned and butterflied
6 thin slices Virginia ham
12 tablespoons onion or garlic Alouette cheese
Wine Sauce
Freshly chopped chives

1. Preheat oven to 350°.
2. Lay the butterflied chicken breasts flat and cover each with 1 slice ham. Top each piece of ham with 2 tablespoons cheese. Roll the ends of the chicken breasts to center, completely enveloping the cheese.
3. Place the breasts in a buttered baking dish. Cover with foil. Bake in preheated oven 45 minutes.
4. Place on a serving platter and spoon hot **Wine Sauce** over. Garnish with chives. Serve the remaining sauce at table.

Wine Sauce

6 tablespoons butter
¼ cup flour
4 cubes chicken bouillon
1¼ cups milk
1 tablespoon fresh lemon juice
⅛ teaspoon freshly ground white pepper
1 tablespoon chopped parsley
½ teaspoon ground nutmeg
¾ cup Chablis or dry white wine

1. Melt the butter in a saucepan over medium heat. Add the flour, stirring constantly.
2. Dissolve the bouillon cubes in ½ cup hot water. Slowly add to the saucepan, stirring constantly.
3. Add the milk, lemon juice, pepper, parsley, nutmeg and wine. Heat a few minutes. Thin with water to desired consistency.

If you can get fresh chicken or that which has never been frozen, the dish will be superior. Be sure to completely seal the cheese inside the chicken breast before cooking it.

Note: The chicken breasts can be assembled through step 2, covered, and refrigerated until baking time. Do this no sooner than the day before cooking. The sauce can be made a few hours before it is to be served and gently reheated over low heat.

RATATOUILLE

2 tablespoons olive oil
1½ cups peeled and cubed (1") eggplant
1 cup sliced zucchini
½ cup cubed (1") onion
½ cup diced (1") green pepper
1 cup canned diced tomatoes in juice
2 teaspoons Worcestershire sauce
¼ teaspoon ground black pepper
1 teaspoon basil
1 teaspoon marjoram
1 teaspoon oregano
1½ teaspoons cornstarch
½ cup black olives
1 cup shredded Swiss cheese

1. Place the oil, vegetables, tomatoes with juice, Worcestershire, pepper and herbs in a large sauté pan. Simmer, stirring occasionally, 1 hour.
2. Preheat oven to 350°.
3. Place the cornstarch in a small jar with several spoonfuls of liquid from the sauté pan. Cover the jar and shake to dissolve the cornstarch. Pour the mixture into the vegetables and stir gently until thickened.
4. Fold in black olives. Pour into a casserole dish and top with the cheese. Place in preheated oven until the cheese melts, about 3 to 5 minutes. Serve immediately.

Note: The Ratatouille can be made 1 hour before serving, placed in a casserole and topped with cheese. Allow it to set at room temperature, then bake about 15 minutes to warm mixture and melt cheese.

Stir the Ratatouille as it cooks so it won't scorch on the bottom. It should be moist, but not soupy, when served.

CREAM PUFFS
with Strawberries and Raspberry Cassis Sauce

1 cup water
6 tablespoons butter
1 cup flour
½ teaspoon salt
¾ cup eggs (4 to 5 large eggs)

1 quart strawberries, washed, hulled and sliced
Whipped cream
Raspberry Cassis Sauce

1. Heat the water and butter in a saucepan until the water boils.
2. Add the flour and salt all at once and stir quickly with a wooden spoon until the batter is stiff, leaves the side of the pan and forms a ball.
3. Add the eggs gradually but quickly, stirring vigorously until combined. A spoon should stand up in the batter.
4. Preheat oven to 400°.
5. Spray a baking sheet with low-water-content oil. Using a regular-size ice cream scoop, place 6 to 7 scoops of batter onto the sheet, placing far apart because the puffs will expand.
6. Immediately place in preheated oven and bake 35 minutes. Remove from oven and cool.
7. To serve, cut the puffs in half horizontally and place the bottoms in each of 6 dessert bowls. Fill with the strawberries and whipped cream. Place the tops over the whipped cream and ladle the sauce over. Serve immediately.

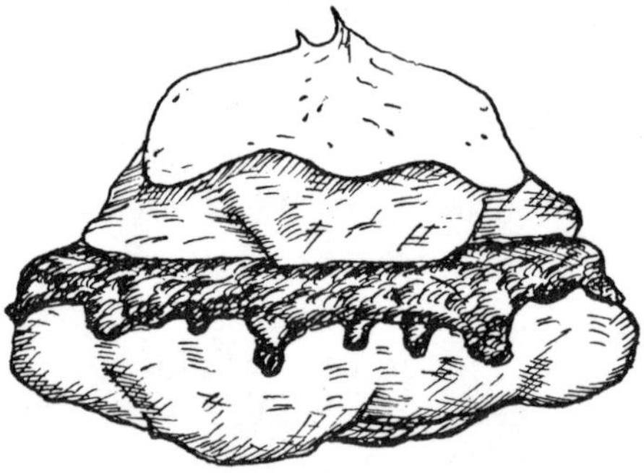

Raspberry Cassis Sauce

1½ cups frozen raspberries in juice, thawed
¼ cup crème de cassis
1 tablespoon sugar

1. Place all ingredients in a blender. Process 1 minute.
2. Strain through a sieve to remove seeds and pulp.
3. Chill before serving.

It is vital when making the cream puffs to quickly stir the batter together. Have all ingredients measured before you start to make the cream puffs. Be sure to strain the sauce to remove seeds and pulp.

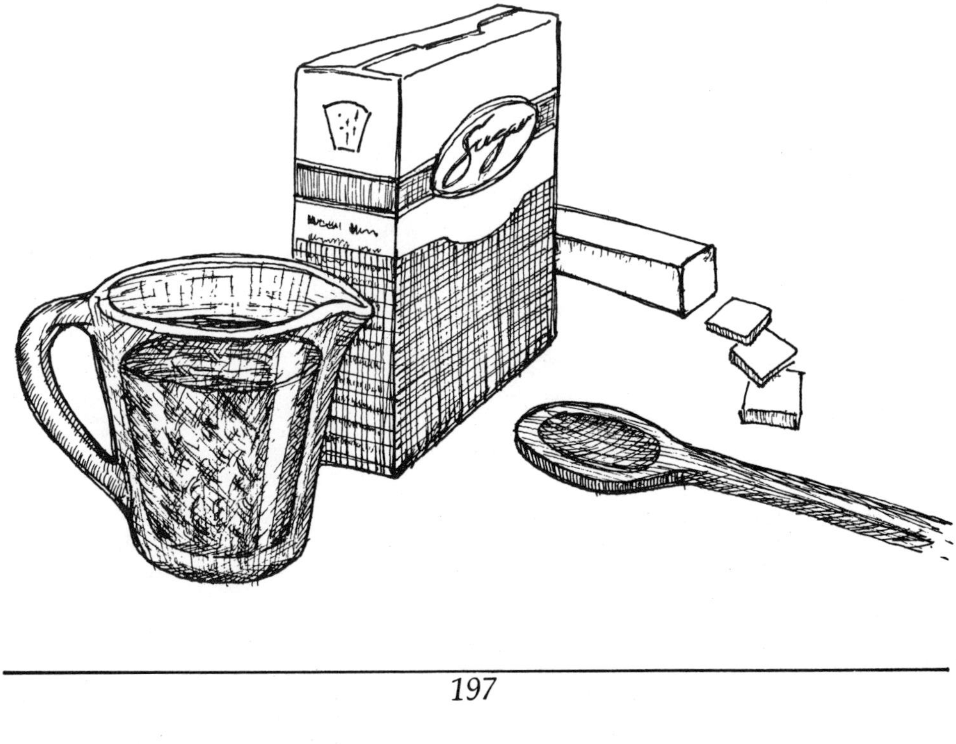

Dinner for Six

Scallops Meunière

Shrimp Bisque

Green Salad with Peppercorn Dressing

Stuffed Trout

Broccoli Hollandaise

Fresh Raspberries with Belgium Sauce

Wine:

With the Scallops–Schloss Vollrads Rhine, Kabinett, 1979
With the Trout–Château St.-Jean Johannisberg Riesling, 1979

Jim Marks, Proprietor
Jon Smith, Chef

RIVER LANE INN

The River Lane Inn is a new restaurant in Milwaukee. Founded in June of 1980, it is doing an admirable job, as quality-and value-conscious Milwaukeeans will attest. The specialties are seafood and fresh-water fish. The emphasis is on freshness—because of this, there is no printed menu. Chef Jon Smith and proprietor Jim Marks work together to select the best-quality seafood, flown in fresh two to three times weekly. The same standard of freshness is applied to all the vegetables served, and Smith and Marks carefully devise their menu to reflect the changing and seasonal varieties of fresh foods.

Another basic tenet at the River Lane Inn is friendliness. "Your first visit to the Inn, you are a customer," says Marks, "By your second visit you are a friend." Marks is there to greet you, seat you and make you feel comfortable, an attitude carried on by the waiting staff.

Marks got his start in the restaurant business when he was fifteen; during college he also worked in a restaurant in which freshness was emphasized. He chose to open a seafood-oriented establishment because he believes it lends itself to more diversified preparation techniques. "Each kind of seafood has its own distinctive style," he observes.

Smith graduated from the Food and Restaurant Program at the Milwaukee Technical College and worked at two well-known Milwaukee restaurants before joining the River Lane Inn. Smith and Marks maintain a staff of fifteen full-time employees, the whole functioning as a closely-knit team.

"A good chef has to be professional, open-minded and always searching for new ideas and dishes. He also must be extremely organized, especially here—when only fresh foods are featured in a restaurant, coordination and timing are critical," Marks asserts.

4313 West River Lane
Brown Deer

SCALLOPS MEUNIERE

1½ pounds bay scallops
4 tablespoons butter
1 clove garlic, minced, or
¼ teaspoon powdered garlic
1 cup chopped mushrooms
¼ cup lemon juice
¼ cup water
¼ cup white wine
Dash of cornstarch
Cooked rice or pasta or toast points

1. Place the scallops, butter and garlic in a sauté pan and cook over high heat until the butter starts to brown, about 3 to 4 minutes.
2. Add the mushrooms, lemon juice, water and wine and cook over medium heat 3 to 4 minutes.
3. Thicken with cornstarch and serve over hot cooked rice, pasta or toast points.

Note: This appetizer can be prepared about 15 minutes in advance of serving. It also can be served as an entrée.

The important part of this recipe is not to overcook the scallops. If you have an electric range, heat the coil before putting the pan on the burner.

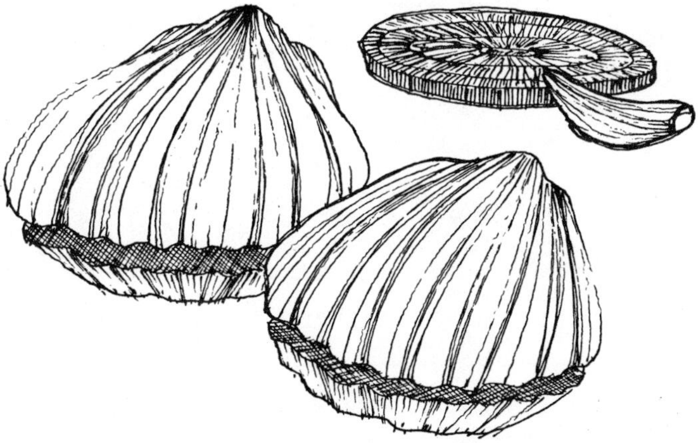

SHRIMP BISQUE

2 cups cream
2 cups Chicken Stock (see index)
½ clove garlic, minced
Dash of salt
Dash of ground white pepper
1 bay leaf
2 cups shrimp, finely chopped
½ cup butter
½ cup finely chopped celery
½ cup finely chopped shallots
½ cup flour
2 tablespoons paprika
½ cup sherry
Chopped parsley for garnish

1. Put the cream, stock, garlic, salt, white pepper and bay leaf in a 2½-quart saucepan and heat. When hot, but not boiling, add the shrimp.
2. Melt the butter in a large pan and sauté celery and shallots; do not brown. Add the flour and paprika and cook 5 minutes, stirring constantly.
3. Remove the bay leaf from the stock and very slowly add the stock to the celery and onions, stirring constantly. Cook until the soup thickens or coats the back of a spoon.
4. Stir in the sherry. Divide among 6 soup bowls. Garnish each bowl with chopped parsley.

Note: The soup can be made in advance through step 3. When reheating, do so over low heat, stirring occasionally.

Don't be afraid to vary this recipe as you gain experience with it.

GREEN SALAD
with Peppercorn Dressing

6 cups fresh salad greens (iceberg, Bibb and romaine lettuces), cleaned and crisped
3 tomatoes, cut into wedges
½ medium-size cucumber, peeled and thinly sliced
½ cup shredded carrot
¼ cup shredded red cabbage
Peppercorn Dressing

1. Put the greens, tomatoes, cucumber, carrot and red cabbage in a large salad bowl.
2. Gradually add the dressing, stopping periodically to toss the salad, until dressed to taste.
3. Divide among 6 salad bowls or plates and serve immediately.

Peppercorn Dressing

2 tablespoons finely chopped shallots
2 tablespoons white vinegar
1¼ cups mayonnaise
¾ teaspoon salt
½ teaspoon garlic powder
¼ cup sour cream
1 tablespoon lemon juice
¼ cup cream or half-and-half
¾ teaspoon Worcestershire sauce
1½ teaspoons freshly ground black pepper
2½ teaspoons cracked black peppercorns
¼ to ½ cup grated Parmesan cheese

Combine all ingredients in a large bowl. Transfer to a jar and refrigerate at least 24 hours before using.

Note: The salad can be prepared through step 1 early in the day. Cover the bowl and refrigerate; dress just before serving.

The Peppercorn Dressing should marinate at least 24 hours for flavors to blend. It can be used on hot vegetables, too, or as a dip for raw vegetables.

STUFFED TROUT

½ cup finely chopped bacon
½ cup finely chopped shallots
½ cup finely chopped mushrooms
½ cup finely chopped celery
1 cup finely chopped crab meat
1 cup finely chopped sole
Pinch of each:
thyme
basil
garlic powder
salt and
ground white pepper
½ cup **Cream Sauce**
12 (6-ounce) fresh rainbow trout
Seasoning salt
4 tablespoons butter, melted (approximately)

1. Sauté the bacon until crisp in a sauté pan. Drain off excess fat.
2. Add the shallots, mushrooms and celery and cook over medium heat 5 minutes. Add the crab meat, sole, herbs and **Cream Sauce.** Stir to mix. Remove from heat and let cool.
3. Preheat oven to 400°.
4. Wash the trout in cold water. Season inside and out with seasoning salt. Place each trout on its side in an 11" non-stick pan and stuff each trout with ½ cup stuffing at room temperature.
5. Put just enough water in the pan to barely cover the bottom. Drizzle the melted butter over the trout.
6. Bake in preheated oven 20 minutes or until done. Serve 2 trout to each person.

Cream Sauce

1 tablespoon butter
1 tablespoon flour
¼ teaspoon salt
⅛ teaspoon ground white pepper
1 cup milk

1. Melt the butter over low heat in a heavy saucepan.
2. Blend in the flour, salt and pepper using a wooden spoon. Cook over low heat, stirring until the mixture is smooth and bubbly.
3. Remove from heat and stir in the milk. Return to heat and bring a boil, stirring constantly. Boil 1 minute.

Note: The stuffing can be prepared in advance and refrigerated until needed. Be sure to bring it to room temperature. The trout should not be cooked until serving time. Remaining Cream Sauce can be covered and refrigerated and used in other recipes.

The important part of this recipe is to have the stuffing at room temperature when stuffing the trout. The idea during cooking is to warm the stuffing and cook the fish.

BROCCOLI HOLLANDAISE

1½ pounds broccoli, leaves removed, cut into uniform lengths

Hollandaise Sauce

1. Put the broccoli in a large pan and cover with water. Cook over medium heat, uncovered, 15 minutes or until the water boils. The broccoli should be firm, yet cooked. Drain and arrange on a serving platter. Keep warm while preparing sauce.
2. Spoon **Hollandaise Sauce** over the cooked broccoli and serve immediately.

Hollandaise Sauce

4 egg yolks
1 pound butter, clarified, or 1¼ cups clarified butter (approximately), very hot
Juice of ½ lemon
8 drops Tabasco sauce
½ teaspoon Worcestershire sauce
¼ teaspoon salt

1. Put the yolks in the top of a double boiler over low heat. Whip constantly and vigorously with a stainless steel whisk. When the yolks begin to set but are still quite wet, remove from heat. This should take 5 to 15 minutes.
2. Slowly add the hot clarified butter, whisking constantly, and alternately adding lemon juice, Tabasco, Worcestershire and salt. The mixture should start to thicken immediately.

Note: If the sauce should separate, add 1 teaspoon boiling water and whisk briskly to bring it back together.

Be sure not to overcook the broccoli. When making the sauce, be sure to cook the yolks a little. This will make the sauce hold together. It's important to add the hot butter alternately with the lemon juice, Tabasco, Worcestershire, and salt. You'll find that the Tabasco gives the sauce a nice flavor touch. Increase the amount of lemon juice if you like a tarter Hollandaise Sauce.

FRESH RASPBERRIES WITH BELGIUM SAUCE

10 egg yolks
1 cup sugar
2 ounces Mandarine Napoleon Liqueur Belgium
1 ounce Grand Marnier liqueur
2 egg whites
2 cups fresh raspberries

1. Place the yolks and sugar in the top of a double boiler over medium heat. Beat until thick, about 7 to 10 minutes.
2. Add the liqueurs and beat until the sauce is thick enough to coat the back of a spoon. Remove from heat.
3. Chill slightly, at least 15 minutes, or until the sauce has the consistency of pudding.
4. Beat the egg whites until stiff, but not too dry. Fold into the chilled mixture.
5. Divide the berries among 6 bowls and cover with Belgium Sauce. Serve immediately.

1 quart hulled fresh strawberries could be used in place of the raspberries; blackberries and peaches are also good. Triple Sec could be substituted for the Grand Mariner. Also, you could stir in finely grated orange or lemon rind if desired. The sauce is also good over blackberries and fresh peaches.

La Rotisserie

Dinner for Four

Crevettes Napoleons

Consommé de Canard

Salade Timbale Rotisserie

Carré d'Agneau Réformé

Pasta d'Épinards

Carrottes Glacés

Fresh Raspberry Ice

Soufflé Arlequin

Wine:

With the Crevettes–Vouvray, 1978
With the Lamb–Stag's Leap Burgundy

Hyatt Hotels Corporation, Proprietor
Wayne Knowles, Executive Chef

La Rotisserie is one of three restaurants within the Hyatt Regency Milwaukee. Its emphasis is on gourmet dining—particularly nouvelle cuisine—and the speciality of the restaurant is roast duck. The intimate restaurant's spacious, comfortable booths, etched glass and fine art overlook the Atrium lobby. Its contemporary design complements that of the entire hotel. Service at La Rotisserie matches the quality of the food: the best.

Subtle sauces and refined simplicity in cooking are the work of Executive Chef Wayne Knowles, who has enjoyed a life-long interest in food. A native of Virginia, he first worked professionally with food while serving in the armed forces. Later he enrolled at the Culinary Institute of America in Hyde Park, New York, graduating in 1969.

"A good chef has patience," Knowles says, adding that he enjoys traveling and talking to people to determine trends in food that can be adapted to La Rotisserie.

"The most difficult part of preparing a meal at home is coordination and timing," claims Knowles. "When the home cook can prepare some dishes in advance of a dinner party, it helps. Then the whole experience can be one of fine dining, accenting the socializing aspect of food. That's what we do in La Rotisserie."

333 West Kilbourn Avenue

CREVETTES NAPOLEONS

8 mushrooms, sliced
8 shrimp, shelled
½ pound crab meat, pressed dry
3 tablespoons butter
1 bunch watercress, cleaned, dried and chopped
1 cup **Sauce Choron**
1 sheet frozen puff pastry, thawed
1 egg, beaten with 2 teaspoons milk

1. Sauté the mushrooms, shrimp and crab meat separately, each in 1 teaspoon butter, until just done.
2. Preheat oven to 350°.
3. In each of 4 (3″ to 4″) straight-sided lightly greased ramekins, alternate one-fourth of the mushrooms, 2 shrimp, one-fourth of the crab meat and one-fourth of the watercress.
4. Divide the sauce among the ramekins. Cut 4 circles out of the puff pastry, each 1″ larger than the diameter of the ramekins. Top the ramekins with pastry circles, pressing the edges of the pastry to the outsides of the ramekins to secure.
5. Brush the egg mixture over the pastry using a pastry brush.
6. Bake in preheated oven 20 minutes or until the pastry is golden brown and crisp. Remove from oven and serve immediately.

Note: This appetizer can be made in advance through step 4.

It is important that the puff pastry adhere to the outside of the ramekins. Simply press it firmly onto the sides of the dish.

Sauce Choron

½ cup clarified butter, hardened
4 egg yolks
2 teaspoons lemon juice or vinegar
2 drops Tabasco sauce
Pinch of salt
2 tablespoons tomato paste

(continued next page)

1. Put one-third of the butter and the egg yolks in the top of a double boiler over hot water. Stir rapidly and constantly until the butter is melted.
2. Add a second third of butter and stir constantly. As the mixture thickens and butter melts, add the last piece of butter, continuing to stir constantly until butter is thoroughly incorporated. Do not let the water over which the sauce is cooking come to a boil.
3. Remove from heat and beat 2 minutes longer. Add the lemon juice or vinegar, Tabasco and salt.
4. Return to heat and beat 2 minutes longer. Remove from heat and stir in the tomato paste.

CONSOMME DE CANARD

½ pound lean ground duck meat
2 shallots, chopped
1 carrot, peeled and diced
1 stalk celery, diced
½ medium-size onion, diced
6 sprigs parsley
6 whole peppercorns
Scant ½ teaspoon aniseed
Scant ½ teaspoon fennel seed
2 egg whites
2 quarts cold **Duck Stock** *or Chicken Stock (see index) skimmed of fat*
1 tablespoon julienned turnip
1 tablespoon julienned leek
1 tablespoon julienned celery

1. Mix the meat, shallots, carrot, celery, onion, parsley, peppercorns, aniseed, fennel seed and egg whites. Place in a 4-quart saucepan.
2. Add the **Duck Stock** or Chicken Stock to the saucepan. Bring to simmer and cook slowly 1 hour. Do not allow to boil or the consommé will become cloudy. Remove from heat. Cool, uncovered.
3. Strain through 2 thicknesses of fine cheesecloth to remove the meat and vegetables and to clarify the broth. Discard the meat and vegetables.
4. Heat the broth to serving temperature. Divide among 4 soup bowls, dividing the julienned turnip, leek and celery evenly among the bowls. Serve immediately.

Duck Stock

Bones from 2 ducks
4 tablespoons duck fat or butter
½ cup chopped carrot
½ cup chopped celery
½ cup chopped onion
8 sprigs parsley
⅛ teaspoon thyme
Scant teaspoon fennel seed
Scant teaspoon aniseed
12 whole black peppercorns
2 quarts water

1. Preheat oven to 350°.
2. Place the duck bones in a roasting pan with 2 tablespoons duck fat or butter. Roast in preheated oven 45 minutes or until the bones are nicely browned. Remove from oven and place in a large soup kettle.
3. Place the carrot, celery and onion in a sauté pan with the remaining 2 tablespoons duck fat or butter and sauté. Add to the soup with the remaining ingredients.
4. Place the kettle over medium heat and bring to a boil. Skim any residue that accumulates on the surface. Reduce heat and simmer 45 minutes. Remove from heat and allow to cool at room temperature, uncovered.
5. Strain through a cheesecloth-lined sieve to eliminate the vegetables, seasonings and bones.

Note: The stock can be made in advance, and may be frozen. The soup can be made in advance through step 3.

Don't omit the anise or fennel seeds from the broth. They add a special flavor. Any variety of vegetables that you like will be fine for the julienne of vegetables added to the broth before it is served. These vegetables do not need to be cooked and are added for color. Obviously, don't include a vegetable like beets because they bleed into the soup, making it look disagreeable.

SALADE TIMBALE ROTISSERIE

2 heads Boston lettuce, washed, drained and crisped
½ cup shredded jicama
1 large or 2 small carrot(s), peeled and shredded
¼ head cabbage, thinly sliced
Creamy Italian Dressing
¼ cup sunflower seeds
1 (2-ounce) package radish sprouts

1. Tear the lettuce into bite-size pieces.
2. Place the lettuce, jicama, carrot and cabbage in a salad bowl.
3. Add dressing and toss to coat. Divide among 4 salad plates, sprinkle with sunflower seeds and garnish with radish sprouts. Serve immediately.

Creamy Italian Dressing

1 egg yolk
1 cup vegetable oil
½ cup plain yogurt
⅛ teaspoon sweet basil
⅛ teaspoon oregano
⅛ teaspoon minced fresh garlic
Salt and feshly ground black pepper to taste
½ green pepper, cored, seeded and liquefied in a blender
½ cucumber, peeled, seeded and liquefied in a blender

1. Lightly beat the egg yolk in a small bowl. Slowly add oil to incorporate.
2. Stir in the yogurt and add the remaining ingredients. Chill before using.

Note: The salad can be prepared in advance through step 2. The dressing can be made well in advance of serving so flavors can blend. Refrigerate the dressing.

CARRE D'AGNEAU REFORME

1 cup olive oil
1 clove garlic, crushed
1 onion, sliced
1 stalk celery, chopped
1 lemon, halved and juiced (save pulp and rind)
½ bunch parsley
1 (8-pound) rack of lamb, trimmed and frenched
2 tablespoons Grey Poupon mustard
½ teaspoon rosemary
¼ teaspoon thyme
4 slices dried white bread, crusts removed, ground into crumbs

1. Combine the olive oil, garlic, onion, celery, lemon juice, lemon pulp and rind and parsley in a deep bowl. Add the lamb rack and refrigerate overnight.
2. Remove the lamb from the marinade and lightly pat dry. Sear over a charcoal fire or in a skillet. (If using a skillet, don't pat the lamb dry; oil from the marinade can be used in searing.) Make sure the meat is well browned. Remove from heat and let cool.
3. Preheat oven to 350°.
4. Brush the lamb with mustard; sprinkle the rosemary and thyme over. Press the bread crumbs into the surface of the lamb.
5. Place in a roasting pan and bake in preheated oven 20 minutes for medium-rare.
6. Remove from the pan and place on a serving platter. Slice at table and serve immediately.

Note: To "french" the rack of lamb is to trim the fat between the rib bones down to where the meat begins, leaving about 2" of exposed rib bones extending out of the meat. Any qualified butcher will be familiar with this procedure.

It is important when seasoning the seared lamb to be sure to cover it completely with mustard, herbs and crumbs.

PASTA D'EPINARDS

¼ pound spinach pasta, cooked according to package directions
2 tablespoons butter, melted

Pour the drained hot pasta into a bowl containing the melted butter. Toss to coat and serve immediately.

CARROTTES GLACES

½ pound carrots, peeled and cut in 1" pieces
2 tablespoons butter

1. Steam the carrots until crisp-tender, 10 to 15 minutes.
2. Place the butter in a skillet and melt over medium heat. Add the steamed carrots and sauté 5 to 7 minutes to heat through and coat with butter. Serve immediately.

FRESH RASPBERRY ICE

1 quart fresh raspberries, crushed
½ cup sugar
¼ cup lemon juice
2 cups champagne

1. Place all the ingredients in a saucepan and bring to a boil. Remove from heat and cool.
2. Pour into a rinsed 1-quart milk carton and freeze.
3. To serve, remove from freezer and wrap in paper. Gently hammer to crush.
4. Place fruit ice in glass dessert bowls or wine glasses and return to freezer until serving time.

Note: This recipe can be made in advance.

Be sure to bring the mixture to a boil to cook the alcohol out of the champagne or the ice won't freeze.

SOUFFLE ARLEQUINE

¾ cup milk
1 (2-inch) piece vanilla bean, or 1½ teaspoons vanilla extract
3 tablespoons butter, melted
6 tablespoons flour
4 eggs, separated
½ cup sugar
Dash of salt
1 tablespoon chopped pineapple
1 tablespoon chopped strawberry
1 tablespoon Grand Marnier
½ ounce sweet dark chocolate, melted
½ ounce bitter dark chocolate, melted
2 tablespoons crème de cacao

1. Heat the milk with the vanilla. Set aside.
2. Combine the butter and flour in a saucepan, mixing until well blended.
3. Remove the vanilla bean from the milk (if used) and add the milk to the butter/flour mixture. Stir vigorously with a wooden spoon, cooking over low heat until the mixture pulls away from the sides of the pan. Remove from heat. The dough will be of cream-puff consistency.
4. Place in a 2-quart mixing bowl and beat in the egg yolks, one at a time, while the dough is hot. Be sure each yolk is thoroughly incorporated before adding another. Add 5 tablespoons sugar, one at a time, mixing after each addition.
5. Preheat oven to 350°.
6. Place the egg whites in a large bowl, add the salt and beat until it forms soft peaks. Add 1 tablespoon sugar and continue beating until the egg whites stand in stiff peaks.
7. Stir 2 tablespoons beaten egg whites into the dough mixture to lighten it. Divide the dough in half and place in 2 bowls.
8. To 1 bowl, add the pineapple, strawberry and Grand Marnier. To the other bowl, add the melted chocolate and crème de cacao.
9. Fold half of the remaining egg white mixture into each bowl.
10. Butter a 1½-quart soufflé dish and sprinkle the bottom and sides with sugar. Place a light cardboard divider down the middle of the dish.
11. Place 1 mixture on each side of the cardboard, then remove the cardboard.
12. Set the soufflé dish in a pan of hot water and place the pan in preheated oven. Bake 50 to 60 minutes or until a toothpick inserted in the center comes out clean.
13. Let the soufflé stand a few minutes. Invert a serving platter over the soufflé dish; turn upside-down to unmold the soufflé. Serve immediately.

INDEX

Appetizers

Beverages

Breads

Desserts and Dessert Accents

Entrées

INDEX

Pasta, Dumplings, Rice, Etc.

Salad Dressings

Salads

Sauces, Stocks and Special Seasonings

INDEX

Soups

Vegetables

DINING IN–THE GREAT CITIES

A Collection of Gourmet Recipes from the Finest Chefs in the Country

---

__044 Dining In—Baltimore 7.95
__041 Dining In—Boston 7.95
__025 Dining In—Chicago 7.95
__027 Dining In—Dallas 7.95
__079 Dining In—Denver 7.95
__045 Dining In—Hawaii 7.95
__024 Dining In—Houston, Vol. I 7.95
__049 Dining In—Houston, Vol. II 7.95
__042 Dining In—Kansas City . . . 7.95
__026 Dining In—Los Angeles . . . 7.95
__092 Dining In—Milwaukee 7.95
__028 Dining In—Minneapolis/St. Paul 7.95
__031 Dining In—Monterey Peninsula 7.95
__038 Dining In—Pittsburgh 7.95
__023 Dining In—Portland 7.95
__033 Dining In—St. Louis 7.95
__020 Dining In—San Francisco . . 7.95
__043 Dining In—Seattle, Vol. II . . 7.95
__078 Dining In—Sun Valley 7.95
__032 Dining In—Toronto 7.95
__056 Dining In—Vancouver, B.C. . 7.95
__064 Feasting In—Atlanta 7.95
__065 Feasting In—New Orleans . 7.95

FORTHCOMING TITLES—SPRING 1982

__091 Dining In—Cleveland 7.95
__083 Dining In—Manhattan 7.95
__046 Dining In—Philadelphia . . . 7.95
__047 Dining In—Phoenix 7.95
__048 Dining In—Washington, D.C. 7.95

☐ CHECK HERE IF YOU WOULD LIKE TO HAVE A DIFFERENT DINING IN–COOKBOOK SENT TO YOU ONCE A MONTH

Payable by MasterCard, Visa or C.O.D. Returnable if not satisfied
$7.95 plus $1.00 postage and handling for each book. MIL 1081

BILL TO:
Name ______
Address ______
City ______ State ______ Zip ______

SHIP TO:
Name ______
Address ______
City ______ State ______ Zip ______

☐ Payment enclosed ☐ Send C.O.D.
☐ Charge
Visa # ______
Exp. Date ______
Mastercard # ______
Exp. Date ______

Signature ______

PEANUT BUTTER PUBLISHING

PEANUT BUTTER TOWERS • 2733 4TH AVENUE SOUTH • SEATTLE, WA 98134